TALES OF THE CRYPTIDS

MYSTERIOUS CREATURES

THAT MAY or may not EXIST

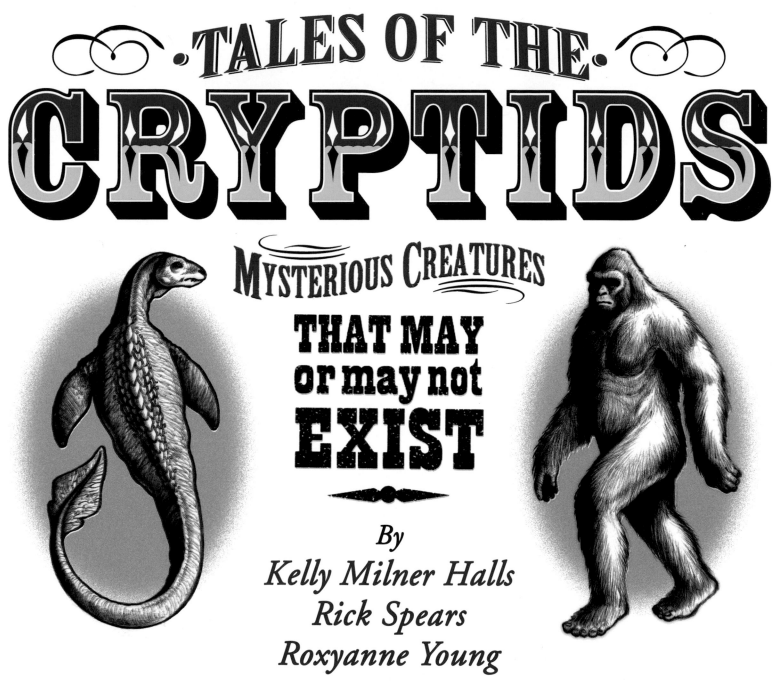

By
Kelly Milner Halls
Rick Spears
Roxyanne Young

DARBY CREEK PUBLISHING

To my daughters Kerry and Vanessa, who keep me from becoming a monster; to the kids and grownups of the Central Valley School District in Spokane, Washington, who helped me stay excited about this project during our school visit days; and to my friend Chris, who taught me to believe.

- KMH

To Matt, Collen, Trenton, Holly, Kara, Ashley, Mr. & Mrs. North America, and all ships at sea.

- RS

To my favorite little monster, Danielle. May you always see the magic and possibilities around you. LYMTA

- RY

Cataloging-in-Publication

Halls, Kelly Milner, 1957-

Tales of the cryptids / by Kelly Milner Halls, Rick Spears, Roxyanne Young ; illustrated by Rick Spears.

p. ; cm.

ISBN-13: 978-1-58196-049-5

ISBN-10: 1-58196-049-2

Includes bibliographical references (p.) and index.

Summary: Cryptozoology is the study of animals that may or may not be real: familiar animals like Bigfoot and the Loch Ness Monster, and those that are less familiar like the Marozi of Kenya, the Orang-pendek of Sumatra and the Thylacine of Tasmania. Meet these and more in this introduction to cryptozoology.

1. Cryptozoology—Juvenile literature. 2. Monsters—Juvenile literature. 3. Animals—Folklore—Juvenile literature. [1. Cryptozoology. 2. Imaginary creatures. 3. Animals—Folklore.] I. Title. II. Author. III. Joint author: Spears, Rick. IV. Joint author: Young, Roxyanne.

QL88.3.H35 2006

001.944 dc22

OCLC: 65184284

DARBY CREEK PUBLISHING

Published by DARBY CREEK PUBLISHING
7858 Industrial Parkway
Plain City, OH 43064
www.darbycreekpublishing.com

5 - BP - 1/1/2010

Tales of the Contents

Crypto-What? 4

A Bigfoot by Any Other Name 7

Sea Serpents Near and Far 23

Mirrors of the Past: Prehistoric Cryptids 37

Cryptic Mammals Uncovered 45

Cryptidictionary 57

Bibliography 67

Index 72

Crypto-What?

Cryp•to•zo•o•lo•gy is one big word that is easily decoded. "Crypto" comes from a Greek word meaning "hidden or covered," and "zoology" is the study of animal life. So, according to the Merriam-Webster dictionary, *cryptozoology* is the study of and searching for legendary animals—called *cryptids*—to find out if there's any possibility that these mysterious animals people say they've seen really exist.

Zoologist Dr. Bernard Heuvelmans (1916–2001) came up with the term. His interest in unproven animal species was as impressive as his study of well-known animals. By 1955, when he wrote *On the Track of Unknown Animals*, Heuvelmans already had been named the father of cryptozoology. Despite his efforts, not everyone in 1955 thought the science was official or real—and the same is true today.

Scientists, including Dr. Michael Voorhies, a paleontologist at the University of Nebraska at Lincoln, are discouraged by the searches for cryptids. "Imaginary monsters are fun," says Dr. Voorhies, "but not nearly as interesting as real living or prehistoric things! And most sightings are easily explained as hoaxes, or misidentifications of well-known things."

Many experts agree with Dr. Voorhies. Even Loren Coleman—director of the International Cryptozoology Museum in Portland, Maine, and an author following in Dr. Heuvelmans's footsteps—admits most sightings prove to be hoaxes or misunderstandings. But Coleman insists that serious scientists are busy at work. And every once in a while, a determined cryptozoologist makes a discovery that knocks the doubtful experts on their ears: proof that one of the legends really does exist. *That* is what keeps crypto-fans searching long after other people have given up.

orang-pendek

coelacanth

In the chapters to come, you will meet some cryptids. In fact, some have been proven to exist. They include:

- **coelacanth:** a real-life fish that didn't realize he was supposed to have gone extinct millions of years ago.
- **Orang-pendek:** a shy, mysterious ape that left enough DNA behind to prove he's more than a legend.
- **giant squid:** a monster-size squid that could take down the average boat, proving that some salty sailors' tall tales may not have been fictional.

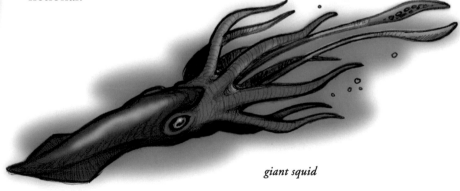

giant squid

But most cryptids are still hidden and unknown, lurking in the shadows of our imagination. Could they make a real-life appearance someday, too?

Why Us? Why Now?

The three of us decided to write a book about animals that may or may not be real for pretty much the same reason. When we were kids, each of us loved the mysterious stories of Bigfoot, the Loch Ness Monster, and other cryptids. So we wrote this book to help you get excited about them, too.

Sometimes the questions we ask are as important as the answers. Imagining what *might* be can open the door to remarkable discoveries in hard science.

Many of these stories may be ones people made up to explain things they didn't understand. But if one or two of the tales turn out to be real, we'll understand life on Earth just a little bit better. And we'll be glad we had the courage to wonder.

We hope you'll have moments of doubt and wonder as you read over this book, because that's the reaction any smart reader *should* have to a book of unsolved mysteries. But remember, life is full of surprises. You never really know what you'll find lurking just around the bend. And here's a bit of truth to send you on your way:

Adventures unfold when you're not afraid to find out.

Kelly Milner Halls
Height: 5' 2"
Shoe size: 6
Favorite cryptid: Albino Sasquatch

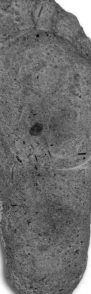

Rick Spears
Height: 5' 9.25"
Shoe size: 10.5
Favorite cryptid: Altie (Altamaha-ha, 'cause it's from Georgia)

Roxyanne Young
Height: 5' 5"
Shoe size: 8.5
Favorite cryptid: Bigfoot, especially the Bardin Booger

Imagine...

...a night as dark as it is quiet—a night wrapped in a blanket of late autumn fog. You're walking home from a friend's house past a stretch of thick, undeveloped forest. You have a flashlight in your hand, and your jacket is pulled tight around you to keep out the damp, evening chill.

Step after step, the only sound you hear is gravel scratching beneath your sneakers. Then a strange howl freezes you in your tracks. A foul odor wafts through the fog, and even though *your* feet aren't moving, you hear something creeping up from behind, snapping twigs and rustling leaves.

You gather all your courage and do a quick about-face to stare eye-level at the belly of a hair-covered giant. You don't see its gentle brown eyes until you look up almost seven feet above the ground. A frightened yelp escapes your open mouth before your hands can cover it.

Startled by your sound, the creature turns faster than you did and, in a panicked gallop, vanishes into the depths of the piney woods. The smell fades slowly, but the memory never will.

You've just seen a Bigfoot.

A Bigfoot by Any Other Name...

Bigfoot. Sasquatch. Yeti. Yeren. Yowie. The names and the details may differ from place to place, but from North America to China to New Zealand, one thing is certain: Something is out there. Chocolate brown or white as snow, these hair-covered, upright-standing creatures have been talked about for more than six hundred years. And whether we read about the ancient legends or the modern-day sightings, the stories make us wonder.

Bigfoot = Sasquatch

Bigfoot is a creature of many names. According to naturalist Dr. Robert Michael Pyle, Native American legends call it by several exotic names, including Sasquatch, Sokqueatl, or Sesquac (from a language spoken by several tribes of Pacific Northwestern Native Americans). No matter how it's pronounced, the name means "wild man."

That certainly describes the creature Roger Patterson and Bob Gimlin claimed they saw wandering along the rural Northern California timberline in October 1967. The creature was enormous—at least seven feet tall—and walked upright like a man. But it wasn't a man. In fact, it was like nothing the outdoorsmen had seen before.

A frame from a film of Bigfoot, taken by Roger Patterson on October 20, 1967, at Bluff Creek, Northern California. Photo Patterson/Gimlin, ©1968 Dahinden

Patterson carefully reached into his saddlebag and pulled out his 16-millimeter movie camera to capture the moment on film. And for decades, Bigfoot believers have been thankful he did.

Was Sasquatch the last thing Patterson expected to see along Bluff Creek as he let his horse rest and sip cool water? Not necessarily. He and Gimlin were known Bigfoot/Sasquatch hunters and longed to prove the legends were true. The film they shot became one of the most famous pieces of footage in Bigfoot history.

Even the experts can't agree on the film's authenticity. Some say it's an elaborate hoax, a fake Bigfoot, a prank. But others see the film as proof-positive that the elusive primate is more than a North American myth.

Cryptid Close-Up

Name: Bigfoot

Other names: Sasquatch, Yeti, Yeren, Yowie, and others

Sighted: Worldwide

Height: 7 to 9 feet tall

Weight: 200 to 300 pounds

Physical characteristics: Biped (walks upright on two feet), eats plants and fruits, is shy and elusive but frequently vocal, and has a strong, unpleasant scent.

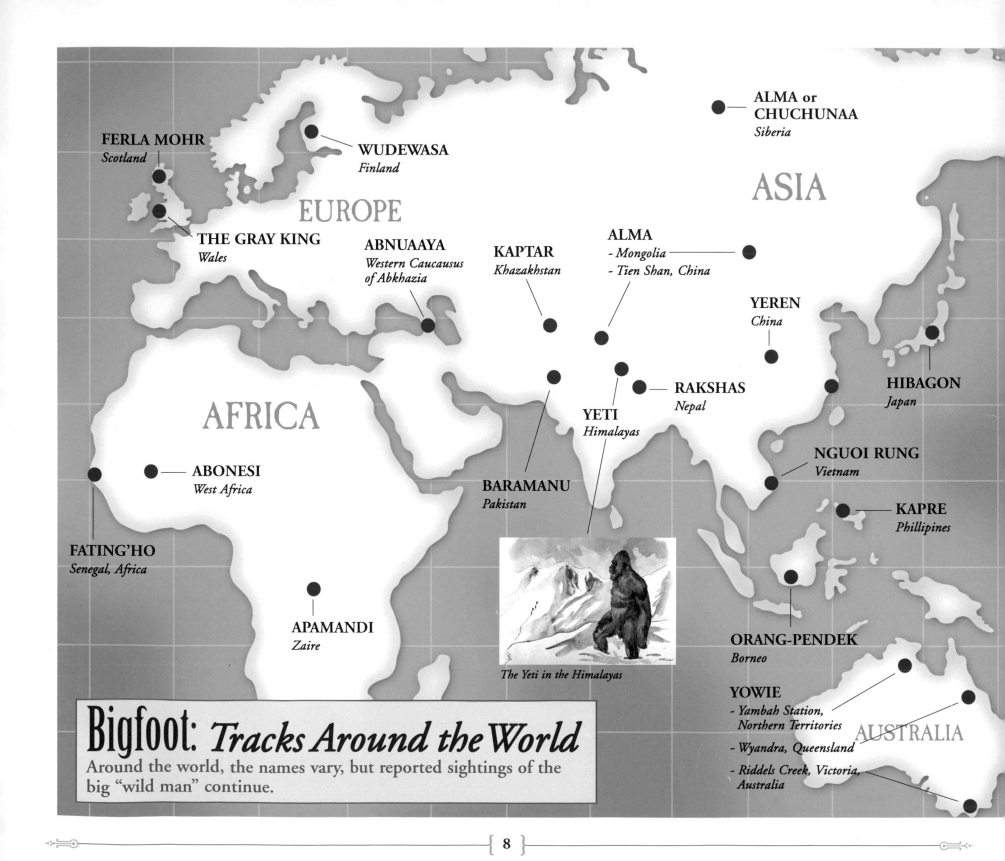

FERLA MOHR
Scotland

WUDEWASA
Finland

ALMA or CHUCHUNAA
Siberia

ASIA

EUROPE

THE GRAY KING
Wales

ABNUAAYA
Western Caucausus of Abkhazia

KAPTAR
Khazakhstan

ALMA
- *Mongolia*
- *Tien Shan, China*

YEREN
China

AFRICA

ABONESI
West Africa

BARAMANU
Pakistan

YETI
Himalayas

RAKSHAS
Nepal

HIBAGON
Japan

NGUOI RUNG
Vietnam

KAPRE
Phillipines

FATING'HO
Senegal, Africa

APAMANDI
Zaire

The Yeti in the Himalayas

ORANG-PENDEK
Borneo

YOWIE
- *Yambah Station, Northern Territories*
- *Wyandra, Queensland*
- *Riddels Creek, Victoria, Australia*

AUSTRALIA

Bigfoot: *Tracks Around the World*
Around the world, the names vary, but reported sightings of the big "wild man" continue.

ARULATAQ
Alaska

TOONIJUK
*Arctic Regions of
North America*

**MANAHA or
WINDIGO**
*Great Lakes Region,
North America*

NORTH
AMERICA

WOOD DEVILS
Appalachia

BARDIN BOOGER
Bardin, Florida

SKUNK APE/MYAKKA
Central and Southern Florida

SWAMP APE
The Everglades, Florida

SASQUATCH

- *Vancouver, Mica Mountain,
  British Columbia, Canada*

- *Mount St. Helens,*
- *Gray's Harbor, Washington*

SOKQUEATL
Eastern Washington

BIGFOOT

- *Pacific Northwest,*
- *Western Canada,*
- *Northern California*

Painting by William M.
Rebsamen, interpreting
Bigfoot/Sasquatch as
Gigantopithecus

**SALVAJE or
VASITRI**
Venezuela

SOUTH
AMERICA

MAPINGUARY
Brazil

UCUMAR
*Andes Mountains,
South America*

*Myakka Skunk Ape:
Man-beast allegedly
photographed in Sarasota
County, Florida, autumn
2000, when it was taking
apples from the back
porch of an elderly
couple's house*

Keeping Track

Dr. Jeffrey Meldrum, Idaho State University Professor of Anatomy, Primatology, and Paleontology

Raised in the heart of Bigfoot country—the Pacific Northwest—Dr. Jeffrey Meldrum grew up in the shadow of the legend. So it's not surprising that he'd have an interest in the hair-covered beast. What makes him different from most Bigfoot-enthusiasts is the careful and scientific approach he's taken to analyze dozens of Sasquatch tracks.

About Dr. Meldrum's research, professor and Cambridge University Press author/editor Walter Hartwig says, "[Meldrum] has executed the model approach. He's weeded out what he believes might be hoaxes or misidentifications. . . . It's beautiful and well-controlled, inductive science. You may think it's far-out, but methodologically speaking, he has toed the line very strictly."

His conclusion? There is sound, scientific reason to believe North America has its own giant ape. But, as he admits in the *Denver Post*, convincing the world and his professional peers hasn't been easy. Meldrum says, "If someone takes the time to visit the lab, they are almost uniformly overwhelmed by the amount of data. Usually they have no concept of the amount of evidence that's been collected."

Dr. Meldrum specializes in the study of bipedalism, *or the ability to walk upright on two feet. This interest drew him into the world of cryptozoology—in particular, into the footprints of the legendary North American ape, commonly referred to as Sasquatch. According to Meldrum, the extensive footprint evidence for this cryptid suggests that is has a flat, flexible foot.*

In 1996, Dr. Meldrum examined fresh footprints firsthand, when he went to an area near the Umatilla National Forest, outside Walla Walla, Washington. There, on a muddy farm road, across a plowed field, and along an irrigation ditch, he found more than 40 separate footprints.

Body of Evidence: *The Skookum Cast*

Using apples and melons as bait, members of the Bigfoot Field Researchers Organization claim to have captured the first partial body cast of a Washington State Sasquatch. Positioned at the center of a mud puddle in the Skookum Meadows of Gifford Pinchot National Forest, not far from Mount Saint Helen's, the tasty snack allegedly convinced a full-grown creature to lie at the puddle's edge and feast. Deep impressions of a hair-covered hip, elbow, heel, wrist, and even buttocks were left in the mud. Mere hours after the mystery creature left the scene, the team captured the impressions in a plaster cast.

Idaho professor Dr. Jeffrey Meldrum, the late Dr. Grover Krantz (a physical anthropologist from the Washington State University), and journalist John Green carefully studied the plaster cast to try to determine what kind of animal actually visited the scene. In a press release circulated by the Idaho State University, the men stated that the impressions could not have been made by any "known" animals living in the region and that an unknown primate was the most likely candidate.

Others have said an elk kneeling to gobble the fruit made the impressions in the mud, not a mysterious cryptid. Dr. Meldrum disagrees.

"While not definitively proving the existence of a species of North American ape," Dr. Meldrum said in the release, "the cast constitutes significant and compelling new evidence that will hopefully stimulate further serious research and investigation."

More than 200 pounds of plaster was used to make the Skookum Cast, which is 3 1/2 feet wide and 5 feet tall. Measurements of the imprints indicated that whatever creature made this impression was 40 to 50 percent larger than a 6-foot-tall human being. When the cast was cleaned, hair samples were extracted. All of them turned out to belong to deer, elk, coyote, and bear—all but one. One hair had unique primate (ape) characteristics. Dr. Henner Fahrenback, a biomedical research scientist from Beaverton, Oregon, has labeled it "Sasquatch."

More details about the cast can be found at the Bigfoot Field Researchers Organization Web site at www.bfro.net.

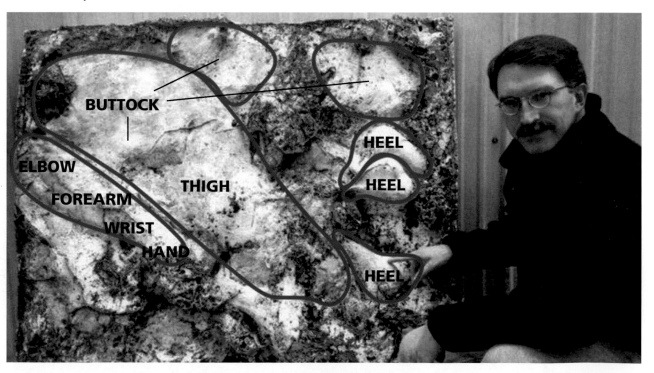

Hair Today, Gone Tomorrow

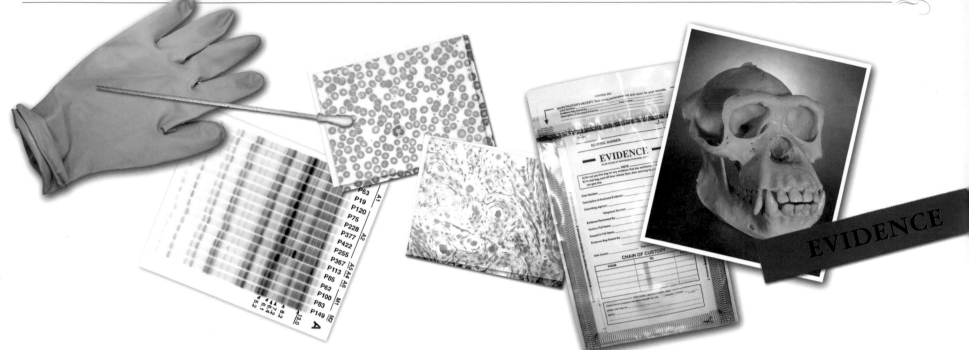

When solving a murder mystery, DNA from hair, fingernails, blood, and body fluids can provide solid proof of "who done it." Unfortunately, hair samples haven't offered much conclusive evidence that Bigfoot exists. Not everyone agrees that the hair from the Skookum Cast offers any real evidence, either.

In July 2005, nine people from Teslin in the Yukon spotted what they called a "bipedal creature" walking nearby. They gathered footprints and a tuft of hair and sent them to their local wildlife expert, who forwarded the hair to Dr. David Coltman, a wildlife geneticist at the Department of Biological Sciences at the University of Alberta, Canada. Later that month, Dr. Coltman tested the sample and found that it came from a bison—perhaps even a bison rug, suggesting it was an intentional hoax.

Although discouraging to the Bigfoot hopefuls, Dr. Coltman offered a glimmer of hope. "While we have shown that this hair sample did not come from an unknown species, such as a Sasquatch," he said, "the faithful can take solace that this finding does not disprove such a species exists."

Albino Sasquatch?

Albinism occurs in nearly all species, including apes and humans.

Reliable statistics show that one in every seventeen thousand human beings is born with albinism. Albinism is a condition that blocks the body's production of pigment so that the person or animal has white skin, hair, scales, feathers, or fur and red eyes. It's not surprising then that people say they've seen this unusual trait among the legendary Sasquatch populations.

Don Keating of Newcomberstown, Ohio, formed the Eastern Ohio Bigfoot Investigation Center after accidentally capturing what he believes was a white Sasquatch on his video camera on August 2, 1992. As he was getting ready to set up in a new location, he left his camera running and caught what he believes were a pair of individuals—one white as snow and one dark brown or black.

In Utah, near a river within the Escalante Wilderness of Garfield County, a hiker reported seeing a "paper-white" mystery animal in June 1996. According to the Bigfoot Field Researchers Organization Web site (www.bfro.net), the creature stood upright on two legs. The hiker and his companion said that the being was between seven and nine feet tall, and it ducked behind rock formations after it realized it had been seen.

In Bailey County, Texas, in November 2001, three men traveling by motorcycle across the five-mile Muleshoe Wildlife Refuge encountered a white Bigfoot and filed a report. According to the Texas Bigfoot Research Center, the first of the three men—who had been of a mile ahead of the others—saw nothing. The second had to swerve off the trail to keep from hitting the strange, white animal that was standing on two feet, but the man didn't get a clear look. The third outdoorsman saw the creature clearly enough to know that white hair covered most of its body and that it had milky-pale skin and red eyes.

Other similar encounters have been reported from around the country—including sightings from Alabama, Illinois, Oregon, Minnesota, Washington State, and Wisconsin.

Yowie Down Under

Australia's native people, the Aborigines, offer up one of the most ancient of the legendary stories. According to their folklore, when Aborigine ancestors migrated to the Land Down Under thousands of years ago, they were met by a ferocious species of ape-men, later called the Yowie, or Doolagahl, meaning "great hairy man." The newcomers triumphed only after they learned to make better weapons than their fearsome foes.

When Europeans began to visit the continent centuries later, they claimed to see the Yowie, too—beginning in the late 1880s. Even modern citizens have claimed their own Yowie sightings, as recently as 1997 in the Tamini Desert of Northern Australia near Alice Springs. According to witnesses, the nearly eight-foot-tall animal had a horrific odor and an odd craving for pipe. It left teeth marks on area waterlines before it tore through some fencing and ran away.

Chocolate Yowie

Capturing a photograph of Yowie may be hard to do in Australia, but capturing a Cadbury Yowie is a piece of cake—make that a piece of *chocolate*.

Since 1997, the world-famous candy maker has sold collectible Yowie chocolate bars for fans for all ages. Buried within the luscious candy goodness are piece-together toy playmates—Yowie friends you can collect and keep. Extremely popular in Australia, they even have their own Web site— http://www.cadbury.com.au/yowie/.

That's one Yowie that's good enough to eat.

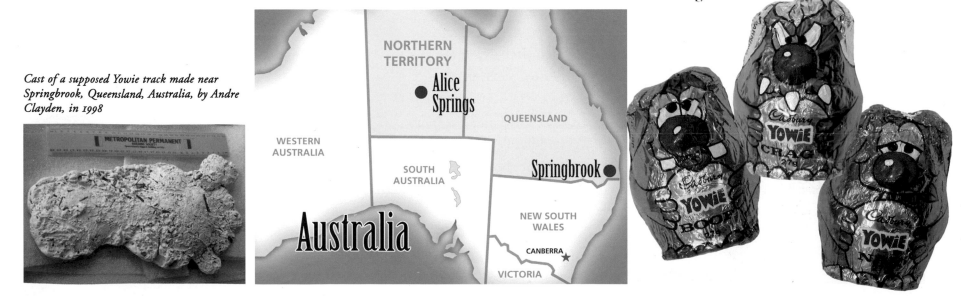

Cast of a supposed Yowie track made near Springbrook, Queensland, Australia, by Andre Clayden, in 1998

Tibetan Yeti

In the mystical land of Tibet in Nepal, high in the Himalayan Mountains, tales of the Yeti, or Abominable Snowman, have been told since the fourth century BC. Covered in hair and as swift as any horse, Yetis have often been reported in pairs, never settling in once place, but moving from territory to territory. They are thought to be clever enough to make useful tools and wise enough to avoid curious humans. Belief in the Yeti among Tibetans is so widespread that the government of Nepal pronounced it "real" in 1961 and named it a national symbol. It is also known as "Rakshasa," which means "demon" in ancient Sanskrit.

Alleged Yeti hand, Nepal

Cryptid Tidbit

Yeti: Also known as the Abominable Snowman, this tall, man-like creature resembles Bigfoot but is known to inhabit only the tallest mountain ranges, such as the Himalayas between India, Nepal, and Tibet. Many sightings by local villagers have been reported through the years, but without documented proof. Some reports say the Yeti is gentle, even helpful. Others paint a more dangerous picture.

Artist's rendering of Yeti

Florida's Skunk Ape

Until the summer of 2004, thirty-two-year-old Florida mother Jennifer Ward didn't believe in Bigfoot—or Skunk Ape, the Floridian nickname for the beast.

"I didn't really think they existed," she said in a November 2004 *Orlando Sentinel* report. But days after hurricane Charley ripped through her county, Ward saw something that would forever change her mind.

Driving down Moore Road in Polk County, she slowed her SUV to focus on what looked like a large animal, nearly eight feet tall, standing upright at a roadside ditch. "I was dumbfounded," she said. "It just watched me as I drove by."

She didn't stop because her two daughters were sleeping in the car, and she was a little afraid. But she is convinced that what she saw was not a bear, despite what some wildlife experts tried to tell her. "No chance at all," she said. She now carries a camera with her wherever she goes—in case she sees the strange creature again.

Scott Marlowe, an archaeologist at the Pangea Institute, who also taught a class in cryptozoology at the Florida Keys Community College, hopes that Ward's encounter turns out to be real, but he admits, "At this point, it's just a single sighting." Until solid evidence—or the Skunk Ape itself—is found, it's just another mystery waiting to be solved.

Could Bigfoot Be *Gigantopithecus Blacki?*

While traveling in Hong Kong in 1935, Ralph von Koenigswald, a German paleoanthropologist—a scientist who studies ancient people and lifestyles—noticed a giant, fossilized molar in a Chinese pharmacy. The medicine man was about to crush the large tooth into a fine powder to create a love potion.

Von Koenigswald retrieved the tooth and later found three more similar teeth during the next four years—teeth he believed came from an undiscovered prehistoric species of man-like ape he called *Gigantopithecus*. When Dr. von Koenigswald was captured and held prisoner by the Japanese during World War II, he had a friend bury the teeth in a milk bottle for safekeeping and allowed another scientist, Franz Weidenreich, to take exact copies to the American Museum of Natural History in New York to study.

By 1946, Weindenreich was convinced that the *Gigantopithecus* teeth were more like human teeth than ape teeth. He believed he and von Koenigswald had found the missing link. But they needed more than four teeth to prove it was a real species. So Chinese scientists Pei Wenzhong and Jia Lanpo continued the search. In 1956, in a single remote limestone cave in Liucheng, China, they found three *Gigantopithecus* jawbones and nearly one thousand teeth. (On the smaller side of things: They later found evidence of a prehistoric dwarf panda, directly related to the modern panda we know today.)

When University of Iowa bioanthropologist Professor Russell L. Ciochon and his team began to study *Gigantopithecus*, they were sure they had an ape, not a prehistoric human. So they hired artist Bill Munns to create a life-size model based on the fossil evidence they had found.

When Bigfoot experts saw Munn's scientifically inspired model, they thought they recognized an old friend. But according to experts, including Professor Ciochon, *Gigantopithecus* went extinct 200,000 years ago during the middle Pleistocene Era, after thriving for nearly six million years in Asia.

(left) Painting by William M. Rebsamen, interpreting Bigfoot/Sasquatch as Gigantopithecus

Could Bigfoot, Yeti, Yowie, or Sasquatch be the modern relatives of *Gigantopithecus*—relics or surviving individuals that somehow escaped extinction? Ciochon says he's received letters from Vietnam-era soldiers who claim to have seen the creature in the wilds of Southeast Asia during the war. And while Ciochon doubts man will ever prove that *Gigantopithecus* still roams Earth, he does like to imagine what it was like when prehistoric man came face to face with the ancient, giant ape.

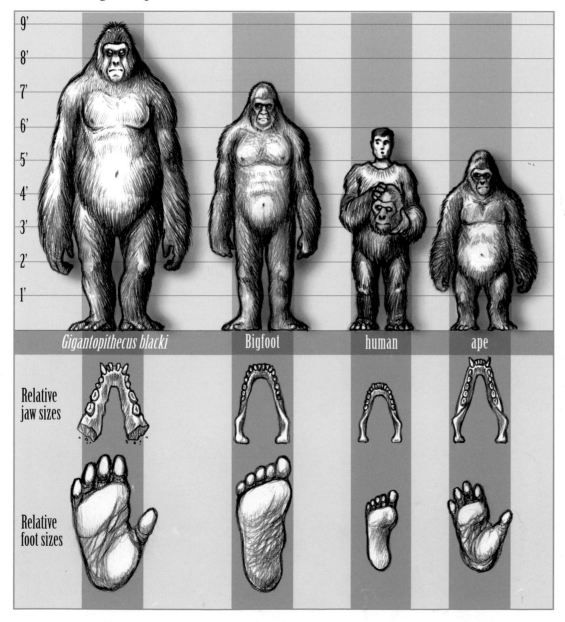

Gigantopithecus blacki   Bigfoot   human   ape

Relative jaw sizes

Relative foot sizes

Artist Bill Munns with his life-size model of Gigantopithecus blacki

A Special-Effects Secret

Special-effects wizards don't normally have "top secret" cryptozoology projects in the works. But Nimba Creations, Ltd., in the United Kingdom is no ordinary special-effects workshop.

Nimba's Creative Director Siobhan Hall and Project Manager Tom Lauten have worked on Peter Jackson's epic movie *King Kong* and Disney's *The Lion, the Witch, and the Wardrobe*. They've made advertisements for Sony's PlayStation2 that look remarkably real. They've even created a make-believe severed head for National Geographic—and a lot more. But none of those amazing credits can compare with what's on their secret drawing board these days.

We caught up with Siobhan Hall to try to gather a few clues. He didn't spill all the beans, but he did tell us a little about their Bigfoot and what might soon be in store. Here's the inside scoop on the project:

Authors: Why did you create your Bigfoot mask?

Hall: Tom and I have had an idea bubbling away in the back of our minds for the last three years regarding a cryptozoology project. It started back in 2001 when we visited Loch Ness on a business trip and discovered just what a spectacular place it was and what a wonderful legend the Loch Ness Monster is—whether you believe in it or not!

Our idea has taken many forms over the years, and it is now very close to being realized—but I can't tell you what it is! However, when it comes to fruition, everyone in the cryptocommunity will hear about it.

We created our Bigfoot bust as a sample of the level of detail that we can apply to such a wonderful creature and which hasn't been explored too often by professional sculptors. But that piece was just a starting point. What we turn out next will really blow you away!

The Bigfoot bust in progress

Authors: Did you base its structure on *Gigantopithecus,* the prehistoric ape?

Hall: We used eyewitness reports, looked at famous images (including the Bluff Creek footage), and also consulted with respected cryptozoologists Lloyd Pie and Loren Coleman to create the piece. We didn't favor one source over another and came up with what we believe to be a reasonable cross-section of opinions to create the piece.

Tom also studied chimpanzee skulls to ensure he had a good starting point for bone structure, which is always important when you are trying to come up with a realistic animal.

Authors: Your mask is so realistic. Do you believe these animals could exist?

Hall: Ahhhhh, the big question! You know, I don't like to ask myself that question too deeply—I think it takes away part of the fun. I'm not really into the idea of arguing with this theory or that theory or debating the evidence with enthusiasts. I'm out to enjoy the rich legend that exists around this and other similar creatures. Would any of us, even the most skeptical people, like to be told that none of these creatures exist for certain? I don't think so. And if you ever had the footage that everybody wanted to see that proved to the world that Bigfoot existed, would you show it to anyone? I think that is a far more intriguing question—and my answer would be NO!

Authors: Is there a place kids can go to see this work in person?

Hall: Right now Bigfoot—which seems to have become our company mascot—sits behind the desk in my office, looking over my shoulder! We have been asked many times for copies for display in various shows, exhibitions, and even films. But for now, we feel we want to keep him as one of a kind.

However, our new project will see a new and more comprehensive version of Bigfoot, which people will be able to get up-close and personal with. Loren Coleman has a crypto-museum in the U.S., and I believe he has some other Bigfoot models, so perhaps that would be a good place for anyone interested to visit and find out more.

For more about Nimba, and updates on their projects, visit their Web site at http://www.nimbacreations.com.

Truth or Fiction?

If Bigfoot does exist, why is it still such a mystery?

According to some experts, it's because these big creatures are nocturnal—they prefer to hunt and socialize after dark. That

makes them much harder to find or even to see. Intellect may have something to do with it, too. If Bigfoot is bright (and most experts suggest that as an advanced primate, it would be), it knows how to hide from man and does so on purpose.

According to world-renowned primatologist Dr. Jane Goodall, when it comes to the possibility of crypto-primates, one should remain "open-minded." She points out that "there is a lot more evidence that they *do* exist" than that they don't.

Why haven't we ever found a Bigfoot body?

It's true that even intelligent, elusive animals die of old age. Why haven't we found a carcass? According to experts at Canada's British Columbia Scientific Cryptozoology Club, it's a matter of climate and biology.

"The reason Sasquatch corpses are not found is probably that most animal carcasses are disposed of by scavengers, ranging from other animals to insects. In many areas where there are purported Sasquatch sightings, the soil conditions are inhospitable for the preservation of remains. From Northern California to Alaska, there is a high acid level in the soil, and this contributes to the rapid decomposition of tissue and bone."

This isn't unusual in nature. Other large predators that we *do* know exist are seldom found after they die. For example, grizzly bears live in substantial numbers in North America, but their bodies are almost never found. Mountain lions are rarely found after they pass away, unless they are hit by cars. And mountain lions are probably not as intelligent as primates.

Remember, there is an interactive ecosystem at work in all natural places. The minute an animal passes away, an army of other animals—from wild dogs to tiny fly larvae (maggots)—gobble up any sign it ever existed. In short order, next to nothing is left behind.

Unsolved Mysteries

So, are the legends true?

The answer depends on which expert you ask. Dr. Russell Ciochon, who has studied the ancient primate *Gigantopithecus*, is doubtful. On the other hand, cryptozoologist Loren Coleman thinks we're on the verge of proving they are. But without DNA evidence from hair, blood, or bones, it's impossible to come up with a conclusive answer either way. So far, no unquestionable Bigfoot DNA has been found. Even so, cryptozoologists will keep searching for the evidence to prove that this creature is not a figment of so many vivid imaginations, but rather is a new species trying hard not to be found.

Even the carcasses of large animals, such as the bear shown here, are seldom found in nature.

Scientists will continue to gather and evaluate evidence of Bigfoot.

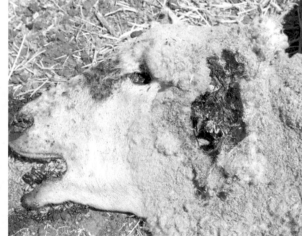

Scavengers depend on the bodies of dead animals to survive. Wolves (right), coyotes, buzzards, and even insect larvae (maggots, above) feed off the remains, and the elements of soil and water gradually break down the hard materials, such as bones and teeth.

Imagine...

...leaping into the waters of a lazy river on a sizzling summer day. You've heard the warnings—campfire stories about a creature that bumped that rickety old pier so hard that a grown man was knocked screaming into the currents. But stories are only stories, so you stick with what's real and take the plunge that will cool you down quickly.

Peacefulness washes over you as you float, refreshed and carefree, down the bubbling stream. Then you feel it—a bump too strong to be a piece of wood drifting in the river. You see your friends frantically waving from the safety of the pier, but you can't quite make out what they're yelling.

Another bump distracts you as you begin to swim toward them, now close enough to hear their terrified screams. "It's behind you! It's behind you!" they yell, pointing and begging you to hurry back to dry land. You think they're just trying to scare you—until you see the diamond-shaped fin break the river's surface, like a living rudder at the end of a ten-foot-long tail.

Could the stories be true?

Sea Serpents Near and Far

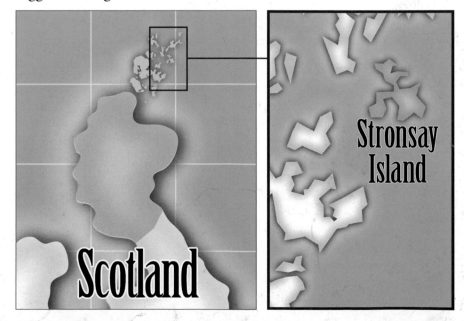

Many scientists believe that graceful but mighty plesiosaurs glided through prehistoric oceans more than 180 million years ago. On the land, *Megalosaurus* might have been the meat-eater most likely to strike fear in the hearts of others, but in the sea, the fish-eating *Plesiosaurus* was king.

According to some experts, these long-necked marine reptiles changed very little over the 135 million years they lived as masters of prehistoric waters. Century after century, era after era, they continued to look the same. So, it's no wonder that the legend-seekers of Scotland's Loch Ness, New York State's Lake Champlain, or other supposed sea-serpent sites worldwide look to the plesiosaurs for answers. If these creatures barely changed during the entire Jurassic era, could it be possible that they live in today's murky waters?

Consider a few of these underwater mysteries—and *you* decide.

The Stronsay Beast

By the time Scottish fishermen John Peace and George Sherar first spotted it on September 25, 1808, the long-necked creature had been dead for days. Seabirds had feasted on the lifeless carcass. Locals had rowed their boats as close as they could get to the jagged rocks and strained to get a good look, but without much luck. Ten days later, a storm washed it up on the Orkneyjar Island beach. Peace, Sherar, and dozens of other villagers stared, wondering what this creature was.

According to one report in *The Orcadian*, the island's newspaper, its flesh was like "coarse, ill-colored beef, entirely covered with fat and tallow." The reporter claimed it looked nothing like a whale or a fish. The skin, he wrote, was "grey-colored and had an elastic texture, two inches thick."

Six "legs" reportedly dangled from the underside of its fifty-five-foot-long body. A wiry mane of silver-colored hair grew from its ten-foot-long neck and shoulders, all the way down to its tail. The mane, according to Orkneyjar Island legends, glowed in the dark, even as the body decomposed.

Four men, including John Peace and George Sherar, examined and measured the body that day. And long after the sea creature had rotted away, their memories were tested—even in a court of law. Island officials took sworn statements from the eyewitnesses, hoping to piece together the facts. Witness Dr. Barclay reported the beast was a new species dubbed *Halsydrus pontoppidani*, after a Norwegian minister known for gathering sea-monster reports in the 1700s. Others said it was a dead basking shark, even though it was fifteen feet longer than the biggest basking shark ever documented.

Scotland

Stronsay Island

The Stronsay Beast: *An Interview*

Dr. Yvonne A. Simpson, Edinburgh University, Geneticist and Writer

Yvonne A. Simpson, a geneticist and writer at Edinburgh University, has spent countless hours researching the facts but remains unconvinced either way. "To decide what the creature may have been," she says, "we must first use clues to rule out the possibilities." Sworn testimony by fishing experts of the day said the animal's skeleton was made of cartilage, not bone. Simpson says this information rules out all mammals, bony fish, and reptiles—including the prehistoric plesiosaur.

Will Simpson offer a guess on what it was? Yes and no. "It seems likely the creature was either a very old basking shark, an unknown shark species, or a completely unknown sea creature," she says. "For now, I am undecided."

More than two centuries have passed since it washed up on shore, and the answer is still unclear.

Dr. Simpson told us why she is interested in the mystery of the Stronsay Beast.

Authors: How long have you been researching sea creatures?

Simpson: I have always been interested in animals and was lucky to grow up in the countryside, where I had access to the sea. I come from a group of islands called Orkney, off the northern coast of Scotland. I spent hours after school each day down at the beach across from Echna Loch, searching in rock pools and seaweed for unusual creatures.

Authors: Why did you decide to invest so much time in this study?

Simpson: I have been interested in cryptozoology since I was a little girl. Everyone has heard of the Loch Ness Monster and the Yeti, but not the Stronsay Beast, which was part of the history of the islands where I grew up. Plus the Stronsay Beast is different from legends, because parts of

Cryptid Close-up

Name: Stronsay Beast

Other names: *Scapasaurus*, name given to two similar carcasses that washed up in 1942

Sighted: Orkneyjar Island, Scotland, on September 25, 1808

Length: 55 feet

Weight: Unknown

Physical characteristics: Serpentine with a neck 10 feet 3 inches long; sheep-like head; gray skin that was "smooth as velvet" when stroked from head to tail but rough when stroked the other direction; six limbs; a mane of wiry hair that glowed in the dark.

its body were and are still available to be examined. Bits of the creature were preserved in jars in the stores of the Royal Museum in Edinburgh. So I wrote to the curator and asked if I could examine the bones.

Authors: What do you believe the Stronsay Beast actually was?

Simpson: That's a tricky question. The more I read and dig into the facts, I only become more certain of what I think it wasn't. We can rule out all the sea creatures that wouldn't be big enough to mistake for the Stronsay Beast. It was huge—16.8 meters long—so that actually narrows down the number of candidates quite a bit.

The remains of the Stronsay Beast are composed of cartilage, not bone. That means all of the animals that have bone can be discounted—mammals and reptiles, such as whales and dinosaurs. We're not looking for a living fossil, for instance.

So if it's none of those listed, then what's left? Fish with skeletons made of cartilage—sharks, rays, and some small groups, such as chimera fish. Based on size, we can rule them all out—except for the sharks. The biggest shark in the world is the whale shark. The biggest whale shark ever recorded was twenty-five meters long. The interviews I held with shark experts ruled out whale sharks because they aren't found around Orkney. And sharks sink when they die, so a dead one wouldn't have floated to Orkney in the currents.

That left me with two possibilities: The creature was either a very badly decayed basking shark of a size much greater than any known basking shark, or it was an unknown type of sea creature.

So the only honest answer I can give you is that I'm not sure what the Stronsay Beast was. But wouldn't it be wonderful if it actually had been a creature unknown to science? If that were really the case, it would support reliable residents of the islands who claim to have witnessed live creatures of a similar shape in the seas nearby.

Dr. Yvonne A. Simpson looks at the pieces of the Stronsay Beast preserved in jars at the Royal Museum in Edinburgh, Scotland.

The basking shark, shown above, is common to the waters near the Orkney Islands.

The Legendary Loch Ness Monster

In the first century AD, the Romans invaded the land that would become Scotland and met a rugged tribe of people called the Picts. The Picts did not write—but they did carve animal pictures in stone. Most of the creatures are still familiar to us today. But one strange beast with a long snout and flippers instead of feet is a mystery. According to some archaeologists, the odd image is evidence of something that has been lurking in Highland waters for hundreds and hundreds of years.

Written accounts of what we know today as the Loch Ness Monster may have started during the sixth century AD. An Irish monk named Saint Columba (521 AD–597 AD) traveled to Scotland to teach the locals about Christianity. In the year 565 AD, between sermons, Saint Columba was said to have waded into the murky waters of Loch Ness to convert a man-killing sea serpent into a shy monster, the one people frequently claim to have seen in modern times. (A "loch" is a lake in Scotland.)

The Loch Ness Monster, or Nessie, has a history that is centuries old. But its popularity didn't really take hold until the early 1930s, when a road was built around the loch's perimeter. Once travelers started using the roadway to get around, the number of documented sightings began to skyrocket. Dozens of times a year, witnesses reported that something was in that water—something unlike anything they'd seen before.

In July 1933, Mr. and Mrs. George Spicer reportedly saw a long-necked animal with a midsection like a snail waddle from the bushes, cross to the road, and sink into the lake on the other side. They sat in their automobile and watched in stunned silence.

Loch Ness Monster, Scotland, photographed from Urquhart Castle by Anthony Shiels, May 21, 1977

Cryptid Close-Up

Name: Loch Ness Monster

Other names: *Nessie*

Sighted: Loch Ness, Scotland

Length: 6 to 30 feet

Weight: Unknown

Physical characteristics: Eel-like or serpentine, grayish, long-necked with a horse-like head, one to three humps, flippers, a long tail, and perhaps even a mane.

A year later, on a bright, moonlit night in January 1934, medical student Arthur Grant said he nearly hit the lake monster with his motorcycle. His report described a "blob" with a small head, a bulky body, four flippered legs, and a long, thick tail. "Knowing something of natural history," he said, "I can say I have never in my life seen an animal that looked like that. It looked like a cross between a plesiosaur and a seal."

According to some theories, in prehistoric times plesiosaurs left the water to lay their eggs, burying them in the sand or soil, as sea turtles do. But plesiosaur expert Mike Everhart says, "Evidence found in South Dakota and Kansas seems to point toward plesiosaurs giving live birth. It is hard to imagine a forty-foot-long plesiosaur struggling up on a beach to lay eggs. Besides having limbs that were unsuitable for travel on land, there are several good physiological reasons (such as overheating and not being able to breathe) that egg-laying probably would not have been possible in plesiosaurs."

Today the sightings continue. Is a monster really swimming in the depths of Loch Ness? Sightings are one thing; evidence is another. And, so far, no evidence has provided an answer to that question.

Cryptid Tidbit

In 1879 a group of schoolchildren playing near the north shore of Loch Ness supposedly saw a creature the color of an elephant coming down the hillside to the loch, its small head turning side to side as it waddled into the water. Over the centuries, hundreds of people have claimed they've seen Nessie—including a member of Parliament.

'Operation Deepscan' at Loch Ness, October 1987: sonar boats in line abreast, scanning the loch in the search for the Loch Ness Monster

Model of Loch Ness Monster at Loch Ness Monster Visitor Centre, Scotland

A North American "Champ"

Lake Champlain was formed ten thousand years ago when an icy glacier slid down the North American continent. Wedged between Vermont and New York, the lake is one hundred miles long and, in places, as much as four hundred feet deep. A perfect home, say cryptid watchers, for a creature named Champ.

Before and during the 1600s, stories of the horned serpent were common among Native American tribes living on both shores of the massive lake: the Iroquois, or Oneida, spoke of the beast from the western (New York) side and the Abenaki and Algonquin from the eastern (Vermont) shore.

Although there is no scientific proof that Champ really does exist, one woman captured an image that rocked the region in July 1977. While swimming with her family on the Vermont side of Lake Champlain, Sandra Mansi saw something rise out of the water and slowly turn its head, as if to examine the countryside. Mansi ran to her car to get her camera and, in a near panic, snapped one picture before pulling her children from the water and making a fast retreat. For years, she hid the picture away for fear of being ridiculed. But when Mansi met Champ researcher, Joseph Zarzinsky, she found the courage to reveal her rare photograph. As a result, the sea monster's popularity hit new heights.

Published in the *New York Times* in June 1981, Mansi's picture captured a clear, better-focused life form than other previous photos had. Her eyewitness account is also considered the best documented sighting of a "sea monster" in history, according to the *Skeptical Inquirer*, a magazine known for disproving popular hoaxes. Even so, they suspect Mansi's photo may be a fake.

Some experts disagree with the magazine's suspicions, but some feel Mansi's report of Champ's length—twelve to fifteen feet—may be overstated by as much as half. If the animal in the photo is real and measures only six to eight feet in length, some known species might explain the image.

NEW YORK **VERMONT**

Samuel de Champlain, the explorer for whom the lake is named, sighted "Champ" in July 1609 and described the creature as a "20 foot serpent thick as a barrel with a head like a horse." To date, more than 300 sightings have been recorded.

Lake Champlain

Length: 125 miles
Width: Maximum of 13 miles
Area: 600 square miles
Depth: Up to 400 feet deep

The photo of Champ taken by Sandra Mansi in July 1977 at Lake Champlain (Vermont side)

Champ experts Joseph Zarzinsky and John Kirk remain convinced, based on Mansi's description and the studied analysis of two photography experts. Both B. Roy Frieden of the Optical Sciences Center at the University of Arizona and Paul H. LeBlond of the Department of Oceanography at the University of British Columbia agree that the photo has not been altered or unreasonably enhanced.

Detailed Champ-sightings have been common for more than four hundred years, so it's no surprise that the animal has been named a protected species. In April 1982, the Vermont House of Representatives passed a law that protects Champ from "any willful act resulting in death, injury, or harassment." By June of that same year, the New York State Senate had passed a similar law, which was backed in April 1983 by the New York State Assembly. Lawmakers couldn't be sure whether Champ was real or an optical illusion, but either way, they weren't willing to take chances. They didn't want people, especially hunters, to think they could kill the mysterious beast. So, by law, they gave Champ protection.

Name: Champ

Other names: None

Sighted: Lake Champlain, Vermont and New York

Length: 15 to 30 feet; some think much smaller: 6 to 8 feet

Weight: Unknown

Physical characteristics: Dark-colored, long-necked, round-bodied creature similar to a prehistoric plesiosaur.

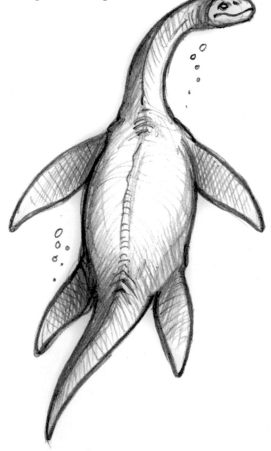

Dozens of Champ sightings have taken place over the past four hundred years, beginning with Samuel de Champlain himself in 1609. This sign lists the names of those who have seen the creature and the date of each sighting.

Could Plesiosaurs Have Survived?

The Stronsay Beast was not a plesiosaur because, according to eyewitnesses, its skeleton was made of cartilage rather than bone. But could other cryptids, such as the Loch Ness Monster and Champ, be prehistoric marine reptiles that somehow escaped extinction?

The experts who oversee the Morden Museum's "Ancient Seas of Manitoba" exhibit and collection in Canada say it's a possibility. The museum's Web site (http://collections.ic.gc.ca/ancientseas/plesiosaurs.htm) states: "It is theoretically possible for a community of animals to live in Loch Ness. They would have space enough; the loch is nine hundred feet deep in places. The loch's immense quantities of salmon would make an ideal food supply."

But the site also points out the problems with the theory. Cold water, roughly forty-two degrees, makes it hard to support the theory that anything reptilian could survive for generations. And plesiosaurs were air-breathing creatures. The Web site explains: "If there were a whole community of creatures in Loch Ness, the surface would be broken several times an hour as the animals rose to breathe." In that case, many more sightings would have occurred by now.

Champ and Whippy: News at Eleven

Sandra Mansi may have the world's best photo of Champ (so far), but Vermont fishermen Dick Affolter and Pete Bodette may have captured the lake creature on digital video.

According to an August 2005 report in the *Burlington Free Press*, Affolter and his son-in-law Bodette were fishing Lake Champlain at the mouth of the Ausable River on July 11 in a twenty-one-foot boat when in the distance they saw something break the surface of the calm water. At first the retired lawyer and fuel business manager thought it was a floating tree trunk or railroad tie. Then it began to move—to swim in what they describe as a "serpentine manner." When they tried to steer the boat closer, the object disappeared. Half an hour later, it broke the water's surface again. This time Bodette and his digital camera were ready—and the mystery was captured on film.

Scientist Steve Smith of the Leahy Center for Lake Champlain's ECHO facilities has seen the footage and says it's difficult to identify what is seen in the video. "I thought I was looking at an otter's nose," he said in a news report.

Affolter isn't convinced they captured images of Champ either, but he says if Smith is right and it's an otter, then it was a *big* one. The creature he filmed was approximately fifteen feet long.

Only a month later, Quebec, Canada, innkeeper Jeff Stafford produced what he called photos of the Lake Massawippi monster affectionately known as Whippy. Tourists staying at his Ripplecove Inn shared their photos with Stafford, saying the ten-foot-long creature that looked like a large water snake or crocodile surfaced head-first, and then stayed visible for several minutes.

According to Canadian Television (CTV), scientists admit that large fish thrive in the five-hundred-foot deep Canadian waters—a seven-foot-long sturgeon has been documented there. But believers insist this was no fish. "It was on the surface of the water for fifteen minutes," Stafford said on CTV. "That's not fish behavior."

A photo of Whippy taken by Jeff Stafford in September 2005

A River's Mystery Monster

We've explored two lake monsters and a mystery from the sea. But have strange creatures been sighted in ordinary rivers? Ask the people of Darien, Georgia, home of the Altamaha River, and the answer from some of them is "yes."

Some reports suggest the monster, dubbed Altamaha-ha, first surfaced along the river in the 1960s. But according to Southern author D. L. Tanner, the Altamaha River monster has a much longer history.

"This thing has been reported for more than two hundred years," says Tanner, quoted in the *Greenville News* in 2003. "It supposedly swims from the ocean up the Altamaha River to Smith Lake. There are dozens of sightings a year."

Sightings include the one reported by three Georgia boys less than a decade ago. Bennett Bacon was only eleven in May 1998—the same age as his friend Rusty Davis. The third boy, Owen Lynch, was twelve. But two years later, they remembered the incident clearly as they talked to *Brunswick News* reporter Jacqueline Bertin on Halloween, October 31, 2000.

Just after Rusty's friend Bennett had jumped into the river for a swim, "this thing popped out of the water," Rusty said. "It was gray and brown, and it had stuff all over it like seaweed and grass." The thing was only ten feet from his friend, who was splashing in the water.

Rusty and Owen screamed for Bennett to get out of the water, but he thought they were kidding—until he turned to see a scaly tail sticking out of the water, so close he could have touched it—if he hadn't been rushing to get out of the water and away from the monster.

Although dozens of other ordinary people swear they've also seen Altamaha-ha, experts at the Georgia Department of Natural Resources insist there is no such thing.

Museum exhibit designer and author/illustrator for this book, Rick Spears isn't quite so skeptical. "I think it's the evolved cousin of a prehistoric whale," he says, "a water-dwelling mammal." Spears created a life-sized, fleshed-out model of Altie (his nickname for the creature). The juvenile Altamaha-ha model is on display in the Rock Eagle Museum of Natural History in Eatonton, Georgia, for all curious visitors to see.

Although no real proof exists that either theory is right—or wrong—Spears believes it's only a matter of time before some evidence settles the question.

Cryptid Close-Up

Name: Altamaha-ha

Other names: Altie

Sighted: Georgia and Florida, beginning in 1969

Length: 15 to 30 feet; a baby about two feet long and a juvenile about twelve feet long (eating fiddler crab in the shallows of a creek) have also been reported.

Weight: 200 to 400 pounds

Physical characteristics: Dark gray or brown, with an alligator-like snout, but the smooth skin of an eel and tire-tread-like ridges on its back; moves up and down like a porpoise, rather than back and forth like a fish; not shy (many sightings claim the creature swims right up next to small boats).

Loch Ness ... Elephants?

Could be! According to a paleontologist at Glasgow University's Hunterian Museum, traveling circuses were popular in Scotland during the 1930s. Dr. Neil Clark's research suggests the circus workers let their elephants swim in Loch Ness to help them relax and exercise between shows. Because most of the sightings in 1933 and after described the creature as gray with a long neck and humped back, Clark feels it is very likely that the onlookers simply saw a bathing elephant.

"When their elephants were allowed to swim in the loch," Clark said in a report on IOL, a South African news Web site, "only the trunk and two humps could be seen: the first hump being the top of the head and the second being the back of the animal. The resulting impression would be of an animal with a long neck and two humps—perhaps more if there was more than one elephant in the water."

The circus owner, Bertram Mills, offered a reward to anyone who could capture the Loch Ness creature for his show. It has been suggested that the elephants were a great marketing scheme, dreamed up after the owner watching one of them swimming in the loch.

Pachyderms or not, many other reported sightings occurred long after the circus was gone—four of them in 2005 alone. Clark believes the later "sightings" have been either hoaxes or misidentifications.

Time will tell if his theory will sink or swim.

True Survivors

The Giant Squid

For decades the giant squid was considered a legend. But in September 2004, a research team found proof near Japan's Bonin Islands—using a remote-control camera to capture more than five hundred images of the twenty-six-foot-long creature trying to take bait from the end of the camera. Tsunemi Kubodera of the National Science Museum in Tokyo and Kyoichi Mori of the Osagawara Whale Watching Association made their discovery public in September 2005.

Many other researchers have gone into depths to try to find the giant squid. Evidence of their reality was solid—usually based on pieces or specimens that were dead or dying. But until these Japanese scientists dove into water so deep that no light penetrated it, no one had been successful.

Cryptid Close-Up

Name: Giant Squid

Other names: None

Sighted: Near Japan, September 2004

Length: Up to 34 feet for males; 44 feet for females.

Weight: Unknown

Physical characteristics: Purplish red; has eight arms covered in tooth-lined suction cups, each one to two inches long; aggressively attacks prey with its enormous tentacles and a sharp beak wide enough to swallow a basketball whole; may have the largest eyes of any living creature: up to a foot in diameter; an organ called a *statocyst* helps it keep its balance (the age of a giant squid can be determined by its number of statocyst growth rings).

Coelacanth

The first fossil record indicates this type of prehistoric fish lived 390 million years ago, and scientists were sure coelacanth had gone extinct sixty-five million years ago. Then, in 1938, a fisherman caught a three-foot-long coelacanth off Comoros Islands near Madagascar. Fifty years later, in 1998, a five-foot-long coelacanth was caught near Indonesia—thousands of miles from the previously discovered colony thriving in the Indian Ocean near Madagascar. "It's a spectacular discovery," said marine biologist Mark Erdman in a BBC news report. "It certainly opens the possibility of all types of other fish and sea monsters that might some day pop up."

Cryptid Close-Up

Name: Coelacanth

Other names: *Latimeria chulumnae*, Gombessa, Mame

Sighted: Near Madagascar and South Africa, 1938; near Indonesia, 1998; a school of 15 with one pregnant female sighted off coast of Sodwana, South Africa, 2002; also Kenya, Tanzania, Mozambique, Comoros, and Sulawesi.

Length: 6 to 26 feet

Weight: Average 175 pounds

Physical characteristics: Closely related to lungfish; has an intercranial joint that allows front and back halves of skull to separate while eating large prey; releases mucus and oil from its rough scales, which are often used as sandpaper; eyes are extremely sensitive to light; seldom active during day or full-moon-lit nights; swims head-down and feeds off ledges.

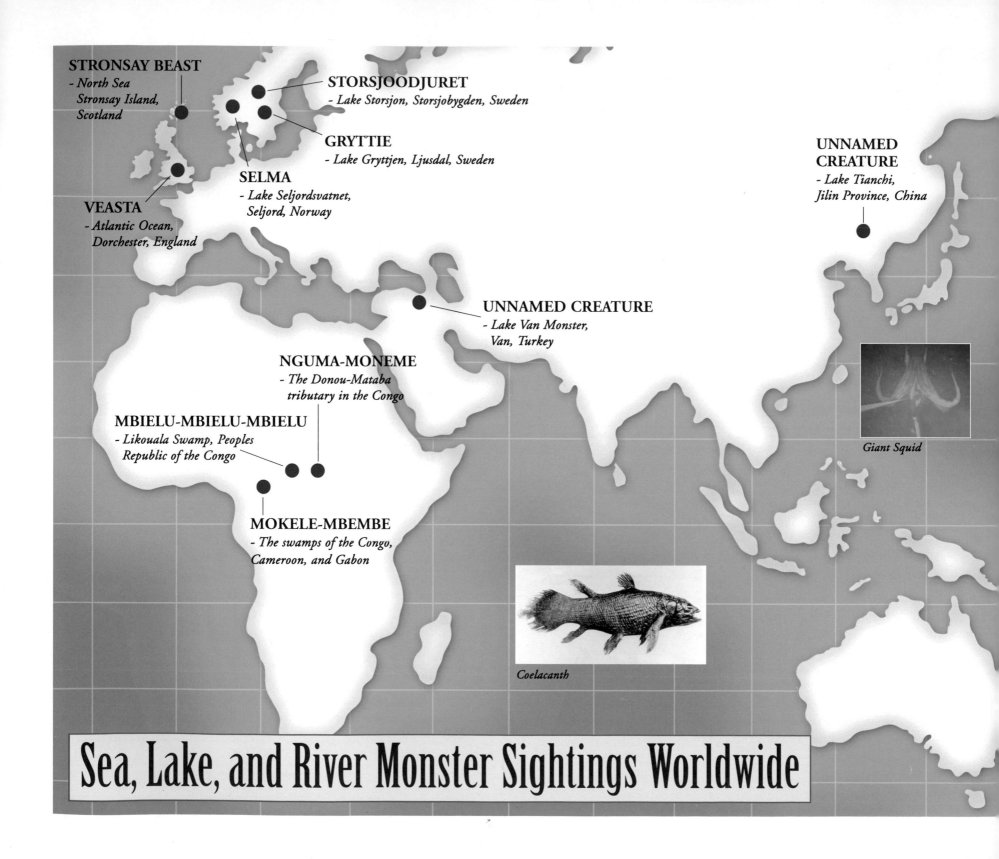

STRONSAY BEAST
- *North Sea Stronsay Island, Scotland*

STORSJOODJURET
- *Lake Storsjon, Storsjobygden, Sweden*

GRYTTIE
- *Lake Gryttjen, Ljusdal, Sweden*

SELMA
- *Lake Seljordsvatnet, Seljord, Norway*

VEASTA
- *Atlantic Ocean, Dorchester, England*

UNNAMED CREATURE
- *Lake Tianchi, Jilin Province, China*

UNNAMED CREATURE
- *Lake Van Monster, Van, Turkey*

NGUMA-MONEME
- *The Donou-Mataba tributary in the Congo*

MBIELU-MBIELU-MBIELU
- *Likouala Swamp, Peoples Republic of the Congo*

MOKELE-MBEMBE
- *The swamps of the Congo, Cameroon, and Gabon*

Giant Squid

Coelacanth

Sea, Lake, and River Monster Sightings Worldwide

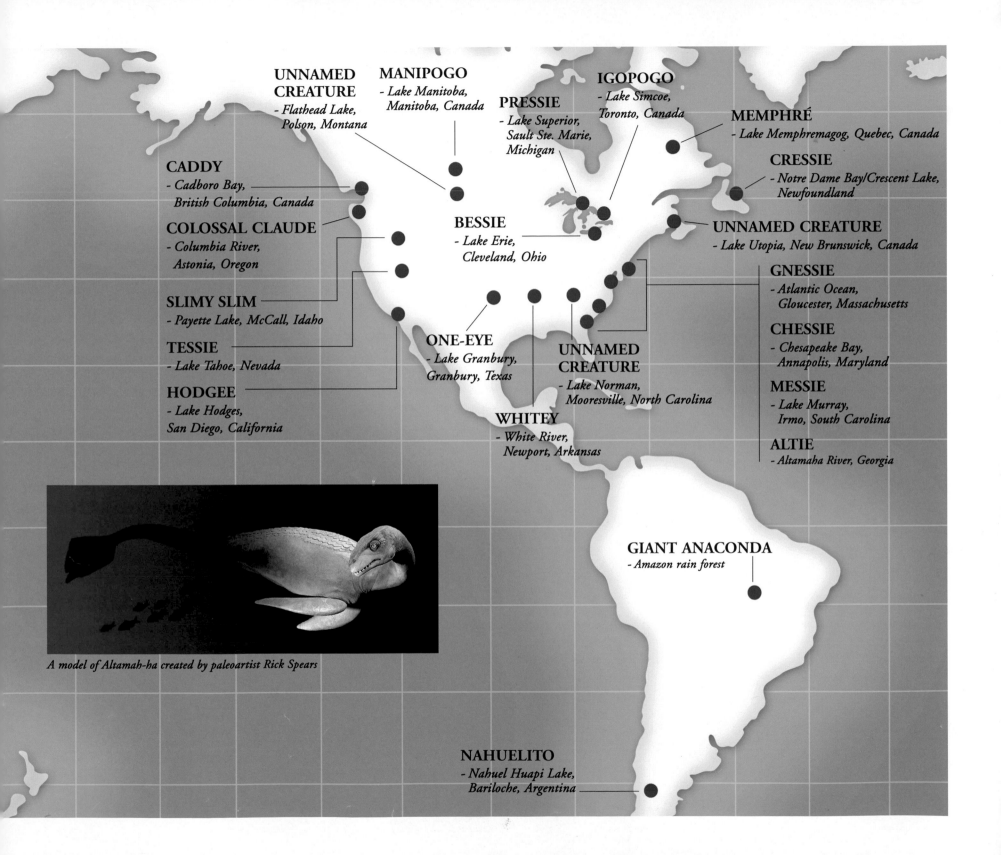

UNNAMED CREATURE
- *Flathead Lake, Polson, Montana*

MANIPOGO
- *Lake Manitoba, Manitoba, Canada*

PRESSIE
- *Lake Superior, Sault Ste. Marie, Michigan*

IGOPOGO
- *Lake Simcoe, Toronto, Canada*

MEMPHRÉ
- *Lake Memphremagog, Quebec, Canada*

CRESSIE
- *Notre Dame Bay/Crescent Lake, Newfoundland*

CADDY
- *Cadboro Bay, British Columbia, Canada*

COLOSSAL CLAUDE
- *Columbia River, Astonia, Oregon*

BESSIE
- *Lake Erie, Cleveland, Ohio*

UNNAMED CREATURE
- *Lake Utopia, New Brunswick, Canada*

SLIMY SLIM
- *Payette Lake, McCall, Idaho*

GNESSIE
- *Atlantic Ocean, Gloucester, Massachusetts*

TESSIE
- *Lake Tahoe, Nevada*

ONE-EYE
- *Lake Granbury, Granbury, Texas*

UNNAMED CREATURE
- *Lake Norman, Mooresville, North Carolina*

CHESSIE
- *Chesapeake Bay, Annapolis, Maryland*

HODGEE
- *Lake Hodges, San Diego, California*

MESSIE
- *Lake Murray, Irmo, South Carolina*

WHITEY
- *White River, Newport, Arkansas*

ALTIE
- *Altamaha River, Georgia*

A model of Altamah-ha created by paleoartist Rick Spears

GIANT ANACONDA
- *Amazon rain forest*

NAHUELITO
- *Nahuel Huapi Lake, Bariloche, Argentina*

Imagine...

... kicking up dust in the heat of central Africa. Your dark brown hiking boots turned red a week ago, stained by the minerals of the soil even before they stopped rubbing blisters on your heels. Your skin turned a deeper brown the week before that.

"Draw it for me," your guide says to the citizens of the Congo who have gathered to find out why you and the other strangers are here. "Show me what the animal looks like," he says again as he hands the tribe elder a pointed stick and points to a smooth place on the ground.

With reverence, the elder murmurs softly in Bantu. Your guide translates in a whisper. "He says they call it 'the one who cuts the flow of water,'" the guide says as the elder etches a head and a long, graceful neck in the mound of dirt. "He says it's more than twenty feet long.'" A thick body and a tail even longer than the neck are added to the drawing.

"A dinosaur," you whisper as the image is almost completed.

A vibration interrupts the elder when he starts the last of four legs—thunder in the distance. The elder begins to speak again as the villagers walk away. Then he follows his people.

"What did he say?" you ask your guide.

"He says the monster speaks to us," the guide translates. "He says it rumbles," he answers, then points, "right over there."

Mirrors of the Past: *Prehistoric Cryptids*

The sea, lake, and river creatures we have already explored are not the only cryptids with a prehistoric look. Travelers from distant lands, especially Africa, have carried with them legends of land-dwelling, dinosaur-like animals. These stories are not as common as the tales of Bigfoot or sea serpents, but they are just as real to the people who tell them—and just as difficult to prove.

Mokele-mbembe, an African Giant

According to CryptoSafari explorer Scott T. Norman, "Mokele-mbembe" means "one that stops the flow of rivers" in the Pygmy languages of central Africa. When Norman traveled to the lands of the Congo, Cameroon, and Gabon in hopes of finding Mokele-mbembe, local villagers drew elaborate pictures to help him visualize what they said they'd seen with their own eyes.

With sticks in the sand, they sketched a huge beast with a long neck and a massive tail. They drew a thick midsection and four stout, sturdy legs—each with three clawed, rounded toes. To the villagers, this was Mokele-mbembe. But to Scott Norman and dinosaur fans worldwide, it was a sauropod—a long-necked, plant-eating dinosaur that went extinct more than sixty-five million years ago.

Could certain dinosaurs in some remote corners of the world have escaped extinction? Most scientists think the idea is simply impossible—but cryptozoologists don't necessarily agree. They wonder about the possibility that evolution took a different path in those hard-to-reach places. In that case, it's possible that modern dinosaur cousins that look a lot like their ancestors could exist. Unfortunately, besides eyewitness accounts, there isn't much evidence to go on. But in the Likouala swamps of the Congo, some people say it's as real as the nose on your face.

CryptoSafari explorer Scott T. Norman and some local people during a search for Mokele-mbembe in Africa

Mokele-mbembe: *An Interview*

Scott T. Norman, President, CryptoSafari

Scott Norman came to his life's calling the way some mysterious discoveries come to light—through a series of curiosities and coincidences. He met one person, who led him to another, who led him to another, and before he knew it, he was building cryptozoology Web sites and planning trips to the Congo. We caught up with him to ask where his cryptid curiosity came from and why he believes there are sauropods in Africa.

Authors: When did you become interested in searching for this cryptid, and how long have you been actively searching for evidence?

Norman: My interest in Mokele has stemmed back to childhood. I've always liked dinosaurs—have never stopped liking them. And the possibility of finding a living dinosaur today is a logical step.

I got involved in cryptozoology and Mokele-mbembe about ten years ago when I was introduced to Herman Regusters, who had been to Lake Tele, Congo, looking for Mokele-mbembe. Herman showed me a video that dealt with his expeditions.

About a year later, I got back into looking for info on Mokele-mbembe and crypto-zoology in general. I started a Web site about Mokele and crypto-zoology, and I started meeting others in the field, including Bill Gibbons, who also had been to Congo looking for Mokele. We were able to successfully mount an expedition to Cameroon in 2001 to look for Mokele-mbembe.

A possible footprint of Mokele-mbembe, showing a sauropod-like shape

Cryptid Close-Up

Name: Mokele-mbembe

Other names: Jago-nini

Sighted: 1932 in Likouala region of the People's Republic of Congo; 1980 on Lake Tele in the Congo; 1981 in the Likouala River near Epena in the Congo; 1983 and 1992 at Lake Tele in the Congo.

Length: Unknown

Weight: Unknown

Physical characteristics: Large, murky, red dish-colored creature with a long neck, round three-toed feet (elephants and hippos have five toes), and a massive tail. It is said to feed on aquatic plants. Some say it has a frilly crest on the top of its head, like a rooster.

Authors: What is the most compelling evidence for or against the Mokele-mbembe being real?

Norman: At this point we don't have any real hard evidence—like a confirmed footprint, DNA sample, or photos— but we do have the testimonies of locals given to me and others that offer strong support for Mokele-mbembe.

We videotaped some interviews with a number of the locals in Cameroon about their experiences.

I was convinced because they talked about the animal as they would about any other animal. They described what Mokele was like and what it ate. One local described how Mokele could eat the leaves off the tops of trees that were around fifty to sixty feet tall. We had a book showing different animals from around the world—modern and prehistoric—and they pointed to the sauropod dinosaur, *Brachiosaurus*.

Authors: What do you think Mokele-mbembe actually is?

Norman: Based on the fact that the locals always picked the picture of the sauropod, I believe Mokele-mbembe is a living sauropod. Another possibility is that it could be an amphibian. But the description doesn't really fit any species of amphibians. And I don't believe that it's a case of mistaken identity. The people in that area know the differences between an elephant and Mokele.

Authors: If it does exist, then how has it escaped being captured on film?

Norman: Like many animals, it doesn't always stick around when people show up. Also, research is not continually going on, so it's hard to photograph an animal when you don't know exactly where it will be. Remember, too, that we were searching the Dja Reserve in Southern Cameroon—that's 1,299,220 acres, including huge areas of swamps and jungle, which are not always easy to navigate.

Scott Norman travels the rivers of the area and rests in man-made huts on his quest to find Mokele-mbembe.

Emela-Ntouka, Horned and Dangerous

Other mysterious animal reports have crept out of the African Congo, including stories of Emela-Ntouka—translation: "elephant killer." Though some cryptozoology fans like to believe this bulky, four-legged animal with a single horn on its nose or forehead could be a ceratopsian (like a *Triceratops*), other theories abound.

Some witnesses say Emela-Ntouka looks like a large, prehistoric rhinoceros—that has adapted to life in the Likouala swamp region. Its long, thrashing tail has been described as crocodile-like. But local villagers say it only eats plants. So why the ferocious name? Some say Emela-Ntouka is cranky and defends its territory—to the death when necessary. If an elephant or other large animal slips into the water in the wrong place, it will face the angry creature's horn of death.

Other accounts give the creature different names. In 1919 a story from Zambia reported in the *London Daily Mail* called the horned animal Chipekwe, or "water rhino." Near Lake Edward in Zaire, it was called Irizima. In Cameroon, it is known as Ngoubu. Regardless of the name, without any proof, such as a living specimen or unaltered photographs or video, the existence of this horned cryptid will remain a mysterious myth, passed down from generation to generation.

Cryptid Close-Up

Name: Emela-Ntouka

Other names: "Killer of elephants," Aseka-moke, Ngamba-namae, Ngoubou

Sighted: Democratic Republic of the Congo, Africa

Length: Slightly longer than an elephant

Weight: Slightly heavier than an elephant

Physical characteristics: Only a little larger than the elephants it reportedly hunts, Emela-Ntouka is said to have a thick tail like a crocodile; brownish-gray, hairless skin; four heavy legs; and three toes on each foot. But its most distinctive physical characteristic is a single, protruding tusk-like horn on its face.

Nguma-Monene, Super-Sized Serpent

Snakes are not unusual in the natural world, but snakes that are 20 to 195 feet long and crow like roosters certainly test the boundaries of our imaginations. Known by local tribesmen as Nguma-Monene (translation: "great snake"), such serpents reportedly swim the waters of the Dongou-Mataba, a tributary of the Ubangi and Mataba Rivers, both of Africa. Eyewitness reports are frequent, even if proof is elusive. Similar snakes are also rumored to slither near the Rio Marmore in the wilds of Brazil in South America.

But are they really river snakes? Or could they be large, plated monitor lizards? Dr. Roy P. Mackal, a University of Chicago zoologist and cryptozoology expert who explored the region in 1986, believes the sightings may be of the latter—large monitor lizards known for swimming long distances to find hearty hunting grounds.

Africa is home to many species of snakes, including the large rock python and the smaller ball python, shown here.

The monitor lizard may be what natives are calling "Nguma-Monene."

Mbielu-Mbielu-Mbielu

A Lizard Living Large

"Mbielu-mbielu-mbielu," roughly translated means "the animal with planks growing out of its back," according to explorer Scott T. Norman. For some people, that description suggests this is a dinosaurian throwback—a strange, modern relative of *Stegosaurus*.

Local villagers, including pygmies, claim that green algae grows on the exposed part of the animal when it surfaces above the water. But they can't be sure how its legs are configured because they have never seen the animal completely out of the water.

Some people even claim Mbielu-Mbielu-Mbielu and Nguma-Monene are the same type of animal. But even those who say they've seen Mbielu-Mbielu-Mbielu, admit they haven't seen it well. So for now, it's another theory that's impossible to prove.

Cryptid Close-Up

Name: Mbielu-Mbielu-Mbielu, "the animal with planks growing out of its back"

Other names: Unknown

Sighted: Likouala Swamp, People's Republic of the Congo

Length: Unknown

Weight: Unknown

Physical characteristics: A large animal living in rivers and lakes with large planks on its back resembling those of a *Stegosaurus*.

Diorama of a Stegosaurus

The Giant Anaconda of South America

In general, the anaconda is the largest snake in the world, not because of its length, but because of it tremendous mass, or weight. But the giant anaconda could be the king of them all.

"Sucuriju Gigante" is the native's name for a giant anaconda, a kind of snake found only in the jungles of South America. During the time of Spanish exploration, some explorers recorded seeing snakes that were more than eighty feet long. They called them *matoras*, or "bull eaters."

Even Bernard Huevelmans, the father of cryptozoology, reported an encounter with a giant anaconda: "What struck me was its enormous head, a triangle about 24 inches by 20. . . . The creature was well over 23 meters (75 feet) long."

Eyewitness reports are one thing; a real-life specimen is another. To date, the largest anaconda ever found was recorded as being about 37 1/2 feet long. Biologist Jesús Rivas has been studying anacondas for more than ten years. He thinks even those recorded to be twenty, thirty, or even forty feet long may have been exaggerated. "In a comprehensive field study involving the capture of more than nine hundred animals," he said, "the largest animals we caught were no longer than nineteen feet." But he adds, "My original data suggests that anacondas may grow to larger sizes in places with more permanent bodies of water." More information about his snaky studies can be found at http://pages.prodigy.net/anaconda/.

So, until a true "giant anaconda" is captured, measured, and hopefully released, the "Sucuriju Gigante" remains on the cryptid list.

Kongamato, Overwhelmer of Boats

Flying reptiles called pterosaurs ruled the prehistoric skies during the Day of the Dinosaur. Experts know they went extinct along with their earthbound counterparts more than sixty-five million years ago. But cryptozoologists say Kongamato might be the exception to that rule.

Reportedly spotted in Zimbabwe, Zambia, Zaire, the Cameroons, and Ghana, these flying Kongamatos (translation: "over-whelmer of boats") supposedly swoop down on unsuspecting fishermen or feed on human flesh by digging up shallow graves. Some African travelers, including Kenyan exchange student Steve Romandi-Menya, say these strange, flying animals are considered commonplace in their homelands. In Zambia, local villagers say Kongamatos may be modern-day relatives of prehistoric bats known as Olitu.

It is possible that this bird, the saddle-billed stork, has been mistaken for Kongamato.

Pterosaur-like flying creatures reportedly seen in Africa, New Guinea, and South America, shown here in an artist's rendering

Cryptid Close-Up

Name: Kongamato, "overwhelmer of boats"

Other names: Olitu, *Pterodactyl*

Sighted: Kenya; near Mount Kilimanjaro, Tanzania; Jiundu Swamps, Mwinilunga District, western Zambia (formerly Rhodesia, in a swamp believed to be the abode of demons); inland swamps of Angola.

Length: Wingspan of 4 to 7 feet; also reported to be the size of an eagle

Weight: Unknown

Physical characteristics: Nocturnal, bat-like creature with large, reddish, leathery, featherless wings; described as a "flying dragon" by Dr. J. L. B. Smith in 1956. Aggressive toward humans.

Imagine...

... the lush underbrush of the Brazilian Amazon, as the sun sinks below the horizon in late afternoon. You are hiking along the steamy banks of the Tapajos River near the village of Barra do Sao Manuel. Moisture from the thick greenery kisses your cheek, your hair, even the back of your hand.

Thoughts of a vanishing rain forest fill your mind, and you nearly miss the first distant cries. But as you continue walking, the screams become impossible to ignore. "What is that?" you whisper, dread stopping you in your tracks. The shrieks sound almost human.

Before the next cry fades away, the smell of rotting flesh attacks your senses, pushing you back a few paces. You pull the collar of your sweat-drenched T-shirt over your mouth and nose and fight back a gag. Then you peer into the thick brush, trying to track the sound to its source in the shadowy distance.

Suddenly you see it—a massive, red, fur-covered arm, clawing toward you defensively. You drop to the ground in fear, just as the animal strikes the trunk of a nearby tree and shards of bark fly in all directions. The creature screams a new warning and carefully stands between you and the reason it's telling you to stay away.

The six-foot-tall mother rears up on her hind feet and howls ferociously, as a small one cowers behind her.

"It's okay, girl," you murmur softly, then slowly back away. "I don't want to hurt your baby."

Could a family of Mapinguari—giant, prehistoric ground sloths—have escaped extinction ten thousand years ago? Could they be hiding in the dwindling rain forests of South America?

Cryptic Mammals Uncovered

Mapinguari—South America's Giant Mystery

Picture an ordinary sloth—a timid, two-foot-long, nocturnal mammal with sharp claws for digging and long, gray fur that is sometimes covered with green algae. Native to rain forests of South America, this barely moving animal gobbles leaves and fruits at night and sleeps at daybreak as it hangs upside-down from a canopy of branches. Hardly fearsome, right?

Now, super-size that sloth. Picture it being six feet tall, standing upright on solid ground, and screeching ominous warnings. Change its fur from gray to red and imagine the horrible stench of garlic and rotting animal flesh. You have just envisioned South America's legendary Mapinguari.

One Brazilian story passed down from generation to generation says Mapinguari is an Amazonian shaman, or medicine man, who discovered the key to immortality hundreds, if not thousands, of years ago. Angry gods punished him for his discovery by turning him into a wandering beast.

Ornithologist—or bird expert—David Oren has studied Mapinguari reports for nearly fifteen years. He doesn't believe the talk of immortality. But after collecting eyewitness reports and video evidence, including claw marks in trees, Oren believes this could be a prehistoric survivor—a giant sloth thought to be extinct for more than 8,500 years.

In the late 1990s, Oren allegedly had twenty-two pounds of hair and droppings analyzed, hoping to solve the mystery at last. But results were hard to confirm. One source said the hair was from an agouti, a rodent similar to but larger than a guinea pig. The fecal samples turned out to be the deposit of a giant anteater. Another source said they indeed belonged to some kind of sloth—but which one?

Experts, including David Oren, remain skeptical. But because the reports are so frequent, they continue to search for proof of the Mapinguari—no matter *what* it turns out to be.

A sloth walking on the ground. Notice the green tint on its fur.

Cryptid Close-Up

Name: Mapinguari

Other names: *Capé-lobo* (wolf's cape), *mão de pilão* (pestle hand), *pé de garrafa* (bottle foot), *juma*

Sighted: Amazon rain forest of Brazil and Bolivia

Height: Approximately six feet tall, but some reports say it can be as tall as nine feet when standing on its hind legs

Weight: Unknown

Physical characteristics: Frightful, red-coated beast of the rainforest, reportedly more than nine feet tall when standing on its hind legs. It has a scream-like cry and razor-sharp claws to rip open the palm trees it eats.

Onza: A Legendary Big Cat Revealed

For centuries in central Mexico, stories were told of a big, golden cat, sleek and aggressive—and unlike the spotted jaguars or pumas native to the region. Thousands claimed to see the mysterious feline prowling the jungles like shadowy beings, always hungry, always hunting.

The Aztecs called it *cuitlamiztli,* and chiseled images of these cats into their stone slabs, walls, and tablets. Emperors, including Montezuma, housed them like rare gems in their private zoos, showing them off to visiting dignitaries.

When the Spaniards arrived, they named the cat Onza, noting how similar it looked to the cougar. But they noted that this stealthy cat was a much better hunter—and it could take down any human challenger not fully prepared for its ferocity. Many powerful Spanish soldiers were caught off-guard by the Onza's powerful strike.

So the old stories go. But without concrete evidence, they were only stories—common, but not necessarily true. Then a Sinaloa rancher shot and killed one of the mysterious animals in 1986. Suddenly experts had the evidence they needed to move the Onza from the fantasy side to the real—but dead—side of the animal map.

According to some reports, the female Onza carcass had a wound on her hind leg, probably inflicted by a warring jaguar. But she still had been a healthy, big cat before her death—able to reproduce in the wild if a male Onza mate existed and was nearby.

Might a male Onza still exist out there, alone? Could cubs be waiting for a mother that will never return? It's hard to say. Even though we now know that the species really exists, the Onza remains a stealthy animal. None have been seen since 1986.

Cryptid Close-Up

Name: Onza

Other names: *Cuitlamiztli*

Sighted: Northwestern Mexico in Sinaloa and Sonora

Length: Approximately 6 feet long from nose to tip of tail (tail may be one-third of its length)

Weight: Approximately 120 pounds

Physical characteristics: Is gold-colored like a puma or cougar, but with longer ears; resembles a wolf; has long, skinny legs and an extremely long tail; has faint striping on lower legs; is aggressive, strong, and dangerous.

Spanish explorers noticed how similar the Onza looked to the cougar (shown at left). Much more aggressive, the Onza also had striping on its legs, while the cougar is golden-colored over its body.

Borophagus or Shunka Warak'in?

Big cats like the Onza aren't the only kind of mammalian cryptid being sought out. From the Big Skies of Montana to the Breadbasket of Nebraska to the wilds of rural Wisconsin, unusual canines have been spotted—strong, bulky wolf-dogs with sharply sloping spines and thick, barrel chests.

Some call this animal the North American hyena. Some say it's *Borophagus*, a prehistoric canine long thought to be extinct. Some even call it the Devil Dog. But the most ancient name seems to be Shunka Warak'in, which in the Ioway Indians' native tongue means "carries off dogs."

Although hundreds of sightings have been reported in the past 250 years, only one specimen has been described in detail. A Montana rancher named Hutchins shot and killed one of the strange beasts. His grandson, Ross Hutchins, allegedly became a zoologist and wrote about the incident in a 1977 memoir. According to the younger Hutchins, the animal was nearly black and looked like a hyena. Its body was donated to a local merchant, who had it mounted by a taxidermist and kept it for several years in his rural Idaho store and museum. No one knows its whereabouts today. But based on the photo, some scientists believe it may have merely been a badly mounted wolf or a peccary, which is a member of the wild boar family.

More recently, in 1997, a Chicago man and his wife allegedly saw a strange, brown, hyena-like animal with white spots on the side of Highway M-29 near the Hiawatha National Forest in Michigan. The animal was about ninety pounds, according to their description. Three years later, the couple reportedly saw another one not far from their home.

Many other similar stories have been recounted. But scientists have some other ideas about these animals' identities. Until another one is found alive—or dead—it remains a mystery.

Hutchins's alleged Shunka Warak'in

Cryptid Close-Up

Name: Shunka Warak'in, "carries off dogs"

Other names: North American hyena, *Borophagus,* Ringdocus

Sighted: Montana and Idaho

Length: About 5 feet

Weight: Unknown

Physical characteristics: Wolf-like, large and dark, with high shoulders and a sloping back like a hyena. One specimen was shot, stuffed, and displayed for many years, but could possibly have been a poorly-mounted or disfigured wolf. Resembles a hyena crossed with a wolf, but cries like a human when hurt.

Bunyip: Cryptid from Down Under

Some say that the Australian continent is a land of rare and unusual animals—and that's easy to prove. All you need to do is look at kangaroos, bilbies, bandicoots, and koalas to be convinced. But what about the Bunyip? You have to look hard in the Land Down Under to find proof of this strange creature.

In Aboriginal bedtime stories, the Bunyip is described as a river spirit that is likely to gobble up children and livestock when they wander too close to the water's edge. The legends tell of a man called Bunyip who broke the Rainbow Serpent's greatest law by eating his totem animals. Banished by the good spirit, Biami, Bunyip became an evil spirit who lured tribesmen and livestock into the waterways where he would eat them. The Bunyip also has been described as a feathered serpent, a swimmer with a dog's head and the flippers of a whale, and even a gopher with the claws of a sloth.

Descriptions change with each retelling, which makes it more likely that the Bunyip is only a vivid fantasy. But this ancient legend, passed down from generation to generation, is a fertile seed in Australia's legendary landscape.

An Australian Aboriginal drawing of a Bunyip made in 1848 in the Murray River area. The animal has a coat either of scales or feathers.

Official postage stamps of Australia depicting the Bunyip in various art styles

Cryptid Close-Up

Name: Bunyip

Other names: *Diprotodon australis*

Sighted: Rivers, lakes, and billabongs throughout Australia, including New South Wales, Victoria, and Australian Capital Territory; most actual sightings were reported in the 1800s.

Length: 4 to 5 feet

Weight: Unknown

Physical characteristics: Varying descriptions include having the body of a calf or a seal and the head of a dog with long fangs and sharp claws; a long-necked, feathered creature with the sharp beak of a bird. Some say it could be a prehistoric rhino, *Diprotodon australis,* that escaped extinction.

Chupacabras: Too Bad to Be True?

In Mexican and Puerto Rican legends, the Chupacabras is a monster—a ferocious beast that drains every drop of blood from its unfortunate victims, often goats and chickens, in record time. They say the vampire-like Chupacabras uses long, sharp fangs to puncture its victim's neck. In fact, the word "Chupacabras" means "the sucker of goats."

The details of each Chupacabras attack seem to change with each so-called witness account. In Chile, a farmer killed a beast that attacked his chickens and called it a Chupacabras. But when experts examined the body, the animal was, in fact, a *yaguarundi*—a wildcat, better known as a jaguar.

Other farmers have killed some hairless Chupacabras that were eating their calves and sheep. But in at least four instances, the monster turned out to be a starving coyote with mange, a skin condition that causes hair to fall out. These creatures, while ugly and desperate to kill in order to survive, are common and not nearly as mysterious as an animal vampire.

Then, in February 2005, target shooters in New Mexico thought they'd found the real thing—a strange, mummified creature that seemed to have wings and fangs. It even had some Hispanic residents whispering, "Chupacabras!" But closer investigation by the New Mexico Game and Fish Office proved that the carcass was that of an ocean skate—a sea creature similar to a stingray. What it was doing in the New Mexico desert was anybody's guess.

Is Chupacabras real? Most experts doubt it. But as long as the legend is real in the minds of so many individuals, the eyes and ears of cryptozoologists—professional and amateur—will be open for discoveries, whatever they turn out to be.

Cast of alleged footprint of Chupacabras, monster of Puerto Rico and Mexico, 1990s, held by investigator Jonathan Downes

Cryptid Close-Up

Name: Chupacabras

Other names: Goat Sucker, El Chupacabras, Elmendorf Beast

Sighted: Puerto Rico, Central America, South America, Mexico, and the southwestern United States—all Hispanic communities, which suggests a cultural phenomenon more than a physical creature

Length: 3 to 4 feet

Weight: Unknown

Physical characteristics: Descriptions vary; a bipedal lizard-like creature with leathery, greenish skin, and wings or sharp spines down its back. It has a face like a dog or panther, a forked tongue, glowing red eyes, and large fangs. Hisses and screeches. Some reports indicate it smells like sulfur; others say it jumps like a kangaroo.

True Survivor: A Peccary Appears

In the 1970s, Ralph Wetzel and some colleagues from the University of Connecticut went to Patagonia, South America, to look for something that had disappeared more than ten thousand years ago: the Chacoan peccary. Two species of peccaries, animals related to pigs and wild boars, were known to exist, but only fossil evidence was found of this, the largest peccary. It had become extinct after the Ice Age. Or had it?

Natives of Patagonia reported seeing the large animal, which they called the tagua. When Wetzel heard the stories, he decided to look for it. And there it was, deep in the forests of South America, alive and well. Science proved it to be the third species because its chromosomes were different from both of the others. The Chacoan peccary is now a protected animal, listed as an endangered species because of its limited population.

South America

Cryptid Close-Up

Name: Chacoan peccary

Other names: None

Sighted: Live specimens have been found in the Gran Chaco region of South America (western Paraguay, northern Argentina, and southeastern Bolivia); documented in 1975, now endangered

Length: About 3 feet

Weight: 66 to 88 pounds

Physical characteristics: A rugged and adaptable wild pig, covered in coarse hair; lives in small, family groups.

A white-lipped baby peccary on the beach   *A collared peccary*

A Hoax ... The Feejee Mermaid Revived

One of the most famous hoaxes in cryptid history is the Feejee (or Fiji) Mermaid. Half-monkey and half-fish, the Feejee Mermaid was supposedly captured near the South Pacific's Fiji Islands in the 1840s. But it was never "real." People, including sideshow promoter P. T. Barnum, tried to convince ticket buyers that it was, and they displayed mummified fakes that had been created to deceive the average person.

"We shall never again . . . woo a mermaid in our dreams," wrote one reporter in the *Charleston Courier* after seeing Barnum's creation, "for the Feejee lady is the very incarnation of ugliness."

Even Barnum agreed, calling the Feejee Mermaid "an ugly, dried-up diminutive specimen . . . its arms thrown up, giving it the appearance of having died in great agony."

Sarina Brewer's Feejee Mermaids are also fakes, one type based on the Barnum creation and another based on designs of her own. Sarina got her degree from the Minneapolis College of Art and Design and considers her work both an art and a science. Her Feejee Mermaids, like the original hoaxes, are created by skillfully blending two parts of unrelated animals into one new being. Sarina's creatures are so expertly prepared that they seem more real than anything P. T. Barnum ever imagined.

"All of my Feejee Mermaids are constructed in a traditional manner similar to the vintage sideshow mermaids," Sarina says. "The exteriors are made entirely of actual animal parts—nothing from a mold. They are absolutely seamless in appearance and are completely convincing, looking like an actual mummified animal."

One of Sarina Brewer's designs—a Feejee Mermaid (right), and Brewer herself with samples of her work (far right)

Sarina says she honors the animals that have passed away by preserving how they looked when they were alive. But she also has the soul of a cryptozoologist—an eye for the mysterious and unknown. "I've always been infatuated with cryptozoology and imaginary creatures," Sarina admits, "but I've also always been interested in sideshows and freaks of nature: cows with two heads, one-eyed piglets, five-legged goats. The Feejee Mermaid is another sideshow staple that people have exhibited forever, so it appealed to me on both levels. Plus I love monkeys!"

How does she make such perfect replicas? That's top-secret! "As closely guarded as Colonel Sanders's eleven herbs 'n' spices," Sarina says. "People try to rip off my trade secrets, so I always need to stay one step ahead of the crowd. Besides, part of the fun is keeping people scratching their heads and rubbing their chins."

Cryptid Close-Up

Name: Feejee Mermaid

Other names: Fiji Mermaid

Sighted: Displayed by P. T. Barnum in New York City in 1842

Length: About 2 feet

Weight: Unknown

Physical characteristics: The torso and head of a monkey and the tail of a fish, all mummified; dark, with arms raised and a pained expression on its face.

(left) This gentle water creature, the manatee, was often mistaken for a mermaid.

(below) Alleged mermaid (made of a stuffed fish and carved wood) on display at the Indian Trading Post gift store in Banff, Alberta, Canada. It is around 3 feet long.

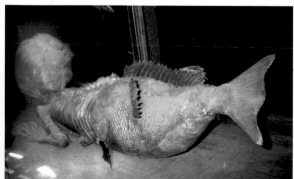

Tales of mermaids are nearly universal. The first known mermaid stories appeared in Assyria, ca. 1000 BCE. Atargatis, the mother of Assyrian queen Semiramis, was a goddess who loved a mortal shepherd and, in the process, killed him. Ashamed, she jumped into a lake to take the form of a fish, but the waters would not conceal her divine nature. Thereafter, she took the form of a mermaid—human above the waist, fish below.

And a Hope: A Tasmanian Mystery At-Large?

Extinction came to the thylacine—commonly called the Tasmanian tiger or Tasmanian wolf—on September 7, 1936, when the last of the breed passed away in Tasmania's Hobart Zoo. All that remained of the once-proud marsupial was a solitary embryo preserved in a jar in the museum (and perhaps a plan to do some DNA cloning someday)—or so they thought.

Enter a German tourist and the pair of color digital photos he allegedly took in January 2005 as he vacationed near Lake St. Clair in central Tasmania, photos even experts can't deny.

"The photographs show what looks to be a thylacine," admitted Environment Minister Steve Kons in a *Sydney Morning Herald* article in March 2005.

"The image to me is clearly of a Tasmanian tiger," said government wildlife biologist Nick Mooney. But both were still skeptical. "The authenticity of the photos is not clear," Mooney continued.

"It's equally possible this could be a hoax," Kon agreed.

The German tourist's brother, who shared the images with a small group of museum and wildlife experts via his laptop, would not allow the photos to be copied in order to remain with officials for further study, perhaps due to copyright concerns.

But Tasmanian museum director Bill Bleathman, who also saw the images, hopes that will change. "It is my hope that he will break his silence and make further contact with the state that the tiger called home."

If the thylacine has escaped extinction, would that be good news? "Oh, it would be extremely exciting for science," Mooney said in an Australian Broadcasting Corporation interview. "I'm not sure what good it might do the species, but it would be extremely exciting for Tasmania as a whole, and Australia and the world would be very excited."

One of the last known photos taken of a thylacine, or Tasmanian wolf, taken at the Hobart Zoo in Tasmania

Cryptid Close-Up

Name: Thylacine

Other names: Tasmanian tiger, Tasmanian wolf

Sighted: Near Lake St. Clair, Tasmania, January 2005

Length: 40-50 inches (about 4 feet)

Weight: Average 33-70 pounds, depending on age and gender

Physical characteristics: A marsupial the size of a wolf, but with stripes like a tiger. Its marsupial pouch is backwards, opening behind rather than forward.

Cryptozoology Today and Tomorrow

Loren Coleman, Cryptozoologist and Author

If there is one person considered to be *the* cryptozoology expert in the United States and around the globe, it's Loren Coleman. Loren has written dozens of books for adults about these mysterious animals. He's appeared on many television documentaries and radio programs. He even runs a cryptozoology museum in New England. And his book for young readers, *So You Want to Be a Cryptozoologist?*, is one of the best guides ever written about investigating crypids.

We caught up with Loren and asked him a few questions about how he found himself in this unusual line of work.

Authors: Did you ever wonder about cryptids when you were a kid? If so, which ones? How were your questions answered as a child?

Coleman: I've been actively involved since 1960, when I was twelve. I'm still a kid in the field at fifty-eight. I wondered about the Abominable Snowmen (Yeti) first. And here's how my questions were answered:

I asked my teachers and was rebuffed. They said, "Don't waste your time." Thank goodness, things have changed today. Then I read everything—articles, books—that I could about the Abominable Snowman. I corresponded with everyone who would answer my questions and would write back. I had four hundred regular correspondents by 1962! I was conducting field investigations, doing cryptid fieldwork, doing original research, and searching old news archives for new discoveries by then. I was fourteen.

Authors: How do you respond to "hard science" experts who say that cryptids are nothing but misidentified, ordinary animal sightings or hoaxes?

Cryptozoologist Loren Coleman with the model known as the Crookston Bigfoot, which is 8 1/2 feet tall

Coleman: I join them and agree. Most reports *are* mistakes or misidentifications, and a few are fakes and hoaxes. But that only accounts for about eighty percent of the cases. We must be open-minded and accepting of the other twenty percent that remain unexplained. That core of cryptids is what keeps me going, what I investigate and/or share with other scientists. (By the way, most cryptozoologists and associates don't wish to be called cryptozoologists.)

I've written about the "ridicule curtain" that surrounds cryptid reports, which keeps most people from comfortably reporting what they see or find, such as footprints. I accept what people bring to me and ask about what or how they are experiencing their sightings and their findings. I start there. I don't make fun of people or of what they say they saw or found. What I eventually discover about their sighting/encounter/evidence should not be biased by any initial, quick, knee-jerk "debunking" of the eyewitnesses due to my thoughts or any scientist's worldview. In that way, I differ from "hardcore skeptics."

One more thing. The "ridicule curtain" comes down during a time of high-volume reporting, as often viewed through the media, as the witnesses' accounts have a context. These "flaps" are important to understand in terms of the press and public acceptance.

Most cryptozoologists are "hard science" people, as we know the value of tangible evidence, of course. But cryptozoologists encompass "soft science" people, too, like folklorists and linguists.

Authors: Which cryptid do you believe we may be close to finding hard evidence for? Why?

Coleman: There seems to be a race on to be the first to verify the next great ape. Physical evidence (foot casts, hair samples, droppings, DNA) is mounting good cases for the Bili (or Bondo) ape of the Congo and the Orang-Pendek of Sumatra. Either one is my best bet for first capture and classification of a new species of ape.

While the "hard evidence" may already be in hand, it appears a higher standard of proof is being demanded with the next great ape discovery—a physical body must be found—than has recently happened with the "verification" of the ivory-billed woodpecker or the new small monkey discoveries in Africa and Brazil. I am openly advocating for a live capture, examination, DNA sampling, photographic record, and release scenario. I remain committed to a non-killing approach to verifying new species. We must stop using the Victorian-style killing of species to "prove" they exist.

Authors: If you could pick one cryptid—and only one cryptid—to find real proof about tomorrow, which one would it be and why?

Coleman: This is a very personal choice, absolutely based on the type of cryptid that attracted me to the field when I was twelve—the Yeti. The fact that I was first interested in Abominable Snowmen and still find it's my favorite, of course, is reflective of the love and special place that these Himalayan hairy hominoids stay in my curious, adventurous, youthful heart, soul, mind, and spirit.

I have done fieldwork in pursuit of Bigfoot, mystery cats, lake monsters, thunderbirds, giant snakes, and numerous other cryptids in every state (except Alaska), as well as Mexico, Canada, and even Scotland (I went to Loch Ness with my sons, Caleb and Malcolm). But my long-term interest in Yeti means that I will feel slightly unfulfilled until I get to Nepal/Tibet someday.

In the End, the Mysteries Remain

Stories have been told, movies have been made, and hoaxes have been exposed. But the mysteries of some creatures remain part of the fascinating fabric of our times.

Consider Mothman. Between November 1966 and November 1967, people in Point Pleasant, West Virginia, say they saw a horrifying sight. A man-sized beast with glowing eyes and huge wings appeared before them. Could it have been a messenger from another realm—or just a large owl with eyes that shone in the night?

Consider the Thetis Lake Monster. Two teenagers ran, terrified, from Lake Thetis in British Columbia, Canada, when they saw a scaly, human-like creature emerge from the water. According to them, the creature chased them, and even cut one of the boys' hands with a sharp fin on its head. The Royal Canadian Mounted Police found the boys so convincing that they launched a huge search for the monster. Four days later, two more witnesses claimed to have seen it. No evidence was ever found.

As you have turned these pages, your head may have been filled with unanswered questions—more questions than you had when you began this cryptic journey. Is Bigfoot real, or just a figment of our imaginations? Could the Loch Ness Monster have been an elephant swimming after a circus performance, or is it a prehistoric whale or an animal we've never seen before? In fact, all of these new questions might leave you feeling a little strange. Just remember this: Some of the most amazing discoveries in science came after hundreds—or even thousands—of questions were asked.

So keep wondering and keep asking questions.

Real or imagined, true or false, you'll find the truth—if you never give up looking for it!

Mothman, the name given to a strange creature sighted many times in the Point Pleasant area of West Virginia

The Japanese fishing boat, Zuiyo-Maru, found a strange carcass in its nets thirty miles east of Christchurch, New Zealand, on April 25, 1977.

Moa were giant flightless birds native to New Zealand.

The first recorded sighting of the Thetis Lake Monster occurred on August 19, 1972, as depicted here.

Cryptidictionary: *An Alphabetic List of Mysterious Creatures That May or May Not Exist*

Cryptozoology is the study of animals that may or may not be real. But are all cryptids as likely to exist as others? Not necessarily. Some creatures that were once considered cryptids have been proven to be hoaxes—total fakes. The good news, though, is that other animals that were once hidden in the shadows of mystery have been scientifically proven to be real. Of course, many cryptids remain unknown, not verified to be either a hoax or a reality.

So, to help you see where each creature falls in the spectrum, we've come up with this Reality Index. Verified real animals get five dots. Verified hoaxes get one dot. And all the others fall somewhere in between, based on the evidence (or lack of it), including eyewitness accounts, photos, footprints, or other data.

Reality Index

• • • • •	**real**
• • • •	**leaning toward real**
• • •	**unknown**
• •	**leaning toward hoax**
•	**hoax**

Of course, we don't know when the next mystery will be solved. But we'll be waiting—watching, reading, and listening. We hope you will, too!

Altamaha-ha • • • •

A mysterious creature that allegedly swims Georgia's Altamaha River. Eyewitness reports suggest it is about twenty feet long and dark-colored with an alligator-like snout, the smooth skin of an eel, and tire-tread-like ridges on its back, and is dark-colored. It is said to move its tail up and down like a porpoise rather than back and forth like a fish. Many eyewitnesses have claimed that the creature swims right up to small boats. The earliest recorded sighting was July 1969, but it was a part of local legends long before then.

Beast of Bodmin Moor • • • •

A black, panther-like creature that roams the United Kingdom. One theory says it's a breed of large cat (seven to nine feet long and two hundred to three hundred pounds) thought to be extinct. Others suggest that a panther escaped from a traveling circus and mated with local cats. More than sixty sightings from Great Britain to Scotland have been reported since 1983, one of which produced a twenty-second-long video.

Bigfoot • • • •

A mysterious primate that has been sighted worldwide and is known by many names, including Sasquatch, Yeti, and Yowie. When hoax master Ray Wallace strapped on wooden feet and left bogus tracks across the backwoods of northern California in 1958, a local newspaper allegedly came up with the term "Bigfoot" to describe the beast that might have made the tracks (before the hoax was revealed). But

Sasquatch, the elusive ape-man of the Pacific Northwest that Wallace was trying to imitate, had been sighted and talked about for centuries before. See *Sasquatch* for more details.

Bunyip • • •

A frightening monster described in Aboriginal legends about a man who broke the Rainbow Serpent's greatest law by eating his totem animals. Banished by the good spirit Biami, Bunyip became an evil spirit that lures tribesmen and livestock into the waterways, where he eats them. Some say it has the body of a calf or a seal, the head of a dog, and long fangs and sharp claws. Others report a long-necked creature with feathers and a sharp, bird-like beak. Some say it could be *Diprotodon australis*, a prehistoric rhino that escaped extinction.

Caddy • • •

A fast, snake-like creature reported to be twenty to seventy feet long. The *Cadborosaurus* of British Columbia's Cadboro Bay (Canada) and other local waters allegedly has humps on its back, flippers like a sea lion, a horse-like head with a mane, and a fan-shaped tail. Clocked doing forty knots in open water, Caddy has been sighted more than two hundred times since the first reports began in the 1930s. Caddy supposedly breathes underwater, which suggests it's not a reptile.

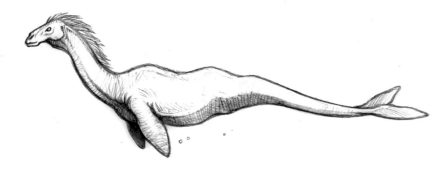

Cardiff Giant •

A ten-foot-tall man of stone once thought to be a Biblical artifact. In October 1869, workers digging a well near Cardiff, New York, made this amazing discovery. People flocked to the area and paid fifty cents apiece to see it—even after George Hull admitted he'd planted the hoax to make a point about taking the Bible too literally. A replica commissioned by circus mogul P. T. Barnum is on display at Marvin's Marvelous Mechanical Museum near Detroit, Michigan. But you can see the original at The Farmer's Museum in Cooperstown, New York.

Chacoan peccary • • • • •

The Chacoan peccary is a wild pig whose discovery was documented by Western science in 1975. Long considered extinct, the Chacoan peccary is now an endangered species living in one of the hottest, driest areas on the planet—the Gran Chaco region of western Paraguay, northern Argentina, and southeastern Bolivia. It lives in small groups of two to ten individuals. These peccaries mainly eat cacti but also enjoy bromeliads (a type of tropical plant) and fruit. The Chacoan peccary's main threat today comes by way of human beings who are clearing land for cattle ranching, over-hunting, and exploring for oil, which affects their environment.

Champ, the Creature of Lake Champlain • • •

A long-necked, round-bodied creature mentioned in Native American legends and documented by European settlers in the 1600s. The fifteen- to thirty-foot-long Champ is often characterized as a prehistoric plesiosaur. Lake Champlain borders both New York and Vermont, and in the early 1980s both states passed resolutions protecting Champ. There have been more than three hundred alleged sightings.

Chupacabras • •

Translated as "sucker of goats," the Chupacabras is said to kill farm animals by draining their blood, supposedly marked by two puncture wounds at the throat. However, eyewitnesses have never documented supposed sightings. Stories of the Chupacabras originated in South America, Mexico, and Puerto Rico among their Spanish-speaking cultures and traveled north with immigrants. It was originally described as alien-like with flexible row of spines down its back, glowing red eyes, and long, sharp fangs. Some reports indicate Chupacabras has wings and smells like sulfur. Others say it jumps like a kangaroo. In more recent days, the creature has taken on more of a dog-like description. In fact, many Chupacabras "discoveries" have turned out to be only sickly dogs that have lost their fur to a disease called mange.

Coelacanth • • • •

One of a colony of the prehistoric *Latimeria chulumnae*, or coelacanth, thought to be extinct for sixty-five million years. In what may be the most amazing fish story ever, a bizarre specimen caught off the coast of South Africa in December 1938 turned out to be a real-life coelacanth. Sixty years later, in 1998, a second colony was discovered. Before this modern rediscovery, the coelacanth was considered to be the link between fish and land-dwelling animals. Closer study revealed that the lungfish is a closer evolutionary match, but coelacanths may still answer questions about how life evolved on our planet. Since their recent discovery, the coelacanth has been named an endangered species, because they are being targeted as catches by fishermen.

Dobhar-chú • • •

A vicious half-dog, half-fish creature living in the lochs of Ireland. Dobhar-chú is sometimes called the "Irish crocodile," although it has no reptilian qualities. Described as a giant, dog-like creature with the head of an otter, it is as big as six large sea otters put together, according to eyewitnesses. It has been said to attack virtually anything near the water's edge. A poem can be found on the gravestone of a woman supposedly killed by a Dobhar-chú in 1722.

Dover Demon • • •

A small, thin, hairless creature with huge paws and feet. Seventeen-year-old Bill Bartlett was driving in Dover, Massachusetts, on the night of April 27, 1977, when he thought he saw a dog or cat in the distance in his headlights. Upon closer inspection, Bill saw an orange-eyed, hairless animal about the size of a goat. Two hours later as John Baker was walking home in Dover, the fifteen-year-old saw what he described as the same creature. The next night, two different teenagers reported sightings. Interestingly, no other appearances have occurred in Massachusetts since. A creature similar to Bartlett's description was allegedly photographed in a park in Chile, but the authenticity of the photo is in question.

Emela-Ntouka • •

A large, single-horned creature living in the same Likoula Swamp region of the Congo as the famed Mokele-mbembe. Emela-Ntouka is slightly larger than a full-grown elephant and has brownish-gray skin, and a long, thick tail. Witnesses reportedly have seen it use its horn to stab and kill elephants during a fight. Emela-Ntouka means "killer of elephants."

Feejee (Fiji) Mermaid •

Was displayed to great fanfare by P. T. Barnum in New York City in 1842. About two feet long, this hoax was actually a mummified torso and head of a monkey sewn to the dried carcass of a fish. Dark, with arms raised and a pained expression on its face, it was described as "the very incarnation of ugliness" by a newspaper correspondent. P. T. Barnum made a fortune showing freaks of nature to eager sideshow goers, and the Fee Jee Mermaid was one of his most popular exhibits. Hardly the beautiful mermaids of legend, these fake mermaids are said to have originated in China.

Giant Octopus • • • •

Not to be confused with the giant squid photographed off the coast of Japan, this cryptid came to light in November 1986 when two boys spotted its carcass on St. Augustine Beach in Florida. Amateur naturalist Dr. DeWitt Webb reported on the mutilated body of a creature that was more than eighteen feet long and had tentacles longer than thirty feet. Webb took tissue samples and photographs for Dr. Addison Verrill, an expert at Yale University. Based on the photos, Verrill believed the creature was a colossal octopus, one hundred and fifty feet long. However, he thought the tissue samples were more likely from a whale. Other scientists studied the samples at the Smithsonian Institute in Washington, D.C., and suggested it could be the tissue of an octopus, a squid, or something completely unknown.

Giant Squid • • • • •

Up until recently, the only proof we had of the giant squid's existence was in the legends of ancient mariners and the scars on whales that eat squid—possibly injuries received in battle. But in September 2004, a Japanese research team using underwater cameras caught video images of a giant squid more than twenty-six feet long. Its beak was big enough to swallow a basketball whole.

Hellhound • • • •

Legendary dogs that supposedly accompany the newly deceased into the afterlife. They are named in various myths worldwide, including Nordic, Indic, Celtic, Germanic, Latin, Armenian, Iranian, Eskimo, Siberian, Greek, and Roman. Hellhounds date back even further to ancient Sumer, where inhabitants worshiped a dog-headed goddess named Bau (as in "bow-wow"). More contemporary hellhounds are described either as large, black dogs with glowing, yellow eyes and bared teeth or smaller, grayish-red dogs.

Jenny Haniver •

These specimens are often presented as proof-positive of mermaids, devils, angels, or dragons, but in reality they're the skeletons and mummified remains of rays and skate fish that have been carved or modified to look different and mysterious, and then preserved with varnish. Originally created by sailors in Antwerp who carved "mermaids" out of dried cuttlefish, these "young girls of Antwerp," or *jeune de Anvers* in French, became "Jenny Hanivers" as they were sold to British sailors and tourists.

The Jersey Devil • •

An early report of this creature originated during America's Revolutionary War. A young New Jersey woman fell in love with a

British soldier, so she was called a traitor. As a result, she allegedly gave birth to a winged devil-baby. Another report says a woman cursed her thirteenth child before it was born. Regardless of its origin, the Jersey Devil allegedly has been sighted many times. Two witnesses who reported seeing it in 1909 described it as three-and-a-half feet tall with a head like a collie and a face like a horse. It had a long neck, wings, and crane-like legs with horses' hooves. Today its greatest claim to fame may be the fact that a hockey team has adopted its name.

Kongamato • •

Deep in the lush tropics of Rhodesia, the natives say a reddish creature with teeth on its back and a four- to seven-foot wingspan (but no feathers) lives. They describe it as a lizard with the wings of a bat. When offered books that include pictures of

birds and pterosaurs—flying prehistoric reptiles—the natives, without exception, point to the pterosaurs and call them "Kongamato."

Kraken • • • •

Norway's natural historians described this giant octopus as a "floating island" with arms long enough to sink a giant warship. It could be a squid or an octopus, but because squid are known to be more aggressive, they seem the most likely match. In fact, on three occasions in the 1930s, squid reportedly attacked ships at sea. The sea creatures were killed when they slid into the moving propellers, but long ago, smaller wooden ships had no such propellers. See *Giant Squid*.

Lake Van Monster • •

In 1995 people along the shores of Lake Van in eastern Turkey saw something long and dark in the water. Researcher Unal Kozak claims to have videotape of the creature from three different sightings of his own. Even so, others are less sure that there really is a water monster, claiming that it's a hoax to bring tourist traffic to this remote area of Turkey.

Loch Ness Monster • • •

The most famous lake creature, Nessie was allegedly first sighted in the sixth century when a monk chastised the creature and ordered it back into the depths. Nessie has reportedly been seen on land, too. A group of 1879 school children playing near the north shore supposedly saw a creature the color of an elephant coming down the hillside to the loch, its small head turning side to side as it waddled into the water. Hundreds of people have claimed to witness Nessie through the centuries, including a Member of Parliament. Recently, the world-famous photo of Nessie has been exposed as a hoax—the photo, not the creature.

Loveland Frog • • •

Few people have witnessed this kind of creature, always late at night on remote back country roads. As a result, it might be easy to dismiss tales of reptilian creatures that stand on two legs and look like frogs, sometimes wielding a weird kind of spark-shooting wand. Some witnesses have reported that the "Loveland Frog" looked right at them before jumping over a guardrail and sliding down the embankment into the Little Miami River near Cincinnati, Ohio. The first sighting was in 1955, and the next ones were almost twenty years later, in 1972, when three separate sightings were reported. Two of the three witnesses were police officers.

Mapinguari • • • •

A giant ground sloth, *Mylodon*, thrived in prehistoric South America before it went extinct eighty-five hundred years ago. But Brazilian natives believe it still exists as a frightful, red-coated beast of the rain forest. Reportedly more than nine feet tall when standing on its hind legs, Mapinguari has a scream-like cry and razor-sharp claws for ripping open the palm trees it eats. Some witnesses believe it could be a giant anteater. The Chacoan peccary—a wild boar thought to be extinct—was found in the deep forests of South America, lending credibility to the possible survival of this sloth.

Marozi • • • •

These spotted lions hunt large game, but allegedly live in the higher altitudes of the Aberdare Mountains of Kenya. Some believe they are a cross between lions and leopards, but experts say that is unlikely. Even if a species crossbreeds, the offspring usually can't produce new litters. It is possible that the spotted coats are a genetic anomaly, like albinism. It is also likely that the animals were juveniles. Some lion cubs are spotted at birth, but lose the markings as they mature. No new reports have surfaced for sixty years, so they may be extinct—if they every existed at all.

Mbielu-Mbielu-Mbielu • •

Another creature of the Congo's Likouala Swamp, this animal is described as large with planks growing from its back like a *Stegosaurus*. It is said to have green algae on its skin because it lives in the lakes and rivers of the region. No witnesses have ever reported seeing it out of the water, so no one knows what its legs or tracks look like.

Megalania • • •

When human beings first entered the inland wilderness of Australia, they encountered the largest goanna lizard of all time, the *Megalania*, or "ancient giant butcher." A distant relative of the modern monitor lizards—including the Komodo dragon—it lived as recently as the Pleistoscene Era (1,600,000 to 40,000 years ago) and ate meat, including mammals, snakes, birds, and other reptiles. But it was as likely to search for dead meat (carrion) as it was to hunt for something living. It grew to a length of about twenty to thirty feet and weighed as much as thirteen hundred pounds, and even though it is thought to have gone extinct, sightings have been reported as recently as 1979.

Megalodon ● ● ● ●

One of the largest predators ever to roam the planet, this prehistoric shark has left behind teeth that are still found in oceans and rock beds around the world. Up to six inches in length, the teeth may have come from a shark that was eighty feet long. That's the same length as two school buses parked end to end. The *Megalodon* is thought to be extinct, but teeth that are only eleven thousand years old reportedly have been discovered. In 1918, Australian fishermen reported a ghostly white shark as long as the wharf they were standing on—115 feet—stealing their three-feet-long crayfish pots—crayfish and all.

Memphré, the Serpent of Lake Memphrémagog ● ● ●

This deep-water lake creature with a long, serpentine neck and humped back reportedly has been seen more than three hundred times in the past two hundred years. It may have been seen much earlier than that, because a Viking pictograph on a mountain above the lake seems to feature the beast. Lake Memphremagog borders both Vermont and Quebec.

Mermaids ● ●

Sailors around the world have allegedly seen or heard mermaids since the first century AD. At first described as having rough, scaly bodies, by the fifth century mermaids became shapely women from the waist up and fish from the waist down. In his ships' logs, Christopher Columbus recorded seeing mermaids. They allegedly rose out of the water alongside his ships, suggesting to marine experts that they may have been dolphins. In 1608, Henry Hudson had a longer encounter with a mermaid off the coast of Russia. He described it as fair-skinned with long, dark hair and a tail like a porpoise, but spotted. In freshwater areas, the gentle manatee may have once been confused as a mermaid.

Moa ● ● ● ●

Picture a forest-dwelling emu or ostrich the size of Sesame Street's Big Bird, and you've imagined the New Zealand giant moa. Now extinct, this flightless bird was likely hunted to death by the indigenous Maori people before 1769, when Captain Cook showed up. Imagine the surprise then, when in 1994 three New Zealanders claimed to have seen one. It may be possible that they escaped extinction after all.

Mokele-mbembe ● ● ●

Deep in the heart of the Congo, which is largely unexplored, the locals talk of a thirty-foot-long, murky-colored creature with a long neck, three-toed feet (elephants and hippos have five toes), and a massive tail. It is said to feed on aquatic plants. Some say it has a frilly crest on the top of its head, like a rooster.

Mongolian Death Worm ● ● ●

Known to the indigenous tribesmen as "Allghoi khorkhoi," or "intestine worm," this blood-red creature with black spots and spiky, horn-like growths on both ends grows to five feet long. It allegedly lives in the vast sand dunes and rocky valleys of the Gobi Desert of Mongolia. Most reports of sightings come during the hottest months of June and July, when the big worm rises from its underground lair. But don't get too close. It supposedly kills from a distance by electric shock or by spitting poison at its victims.

Mothman • • •

On November 12, 1966, five men were digging a grave near Point Pleasant, West Virginia, when a creature that looked like a six- to seven-foot-tall man with wings allegedly lifted off from a nearby tree and flew over their heads. In a year's time, more than one hundred people reportedly had seen it. Each described a large, screeching, gray-brown creature with the body of a man, gliding wings like a bat's, and glowing red eyes, like bicycle reflectors. Many of the sightings were coupled with unusual red lights in the sky, suggesting the Mothman may have been extraterrestrial—from a UFO.

Nandi Bear • • • •

Africa has an amazing variety of wildlife, but bears aren't among them, unless you count this cryptid. Reports of this predatory creature—part bear, part hyena—come from along the River Tana in eastern Kenya. Reportedly a vicious hunter, it comes out at night and targets solitary people or animals. The Nandi Bear is reputedly fond of eating brains, and a local farmer reported more than sixty of her sheep were killed in this manner; however, after hunting down this killer, it was discovered to be a large hyena. Even so, descriptions of a large, furry beast that walks like a bear and can stand upright or sit on its haunches makes cryptozoologists wonder what it might really be.

Nguma-Monene • • • •

A large, python-like creature with a serrated ridge running down its back like a crocodile, but with a forked tongue like a snake and no legs. It has been reported to be between 130 and 195 feet long. That's almost as long as five school buses! "Nguma-Monene" is Lingala for "large python." It reportedly lives in the Dongou-Mataba River region of The People's Republic of the Congo.

Ogopogo • • •

Ogopogos allegedly swim in pairs in the waters of British Columbia. Sighted in Lake Okanagan, they reportedly are thirty to one hundred feet long. Some experts think they might be round-bodied, prehistoric whales *Zeuglodon* or *Basilosaurus*. But how did ocean-dwelling whales wind up in a freshwater lake? Some theorize that they followed tasty salmon upstream and adapted to the cold waters of Lake Okanagan—as deep as eight hundred feet in places.

Onza • • • •

A type of mountain lion prowling the jungles and rocky mountain wilderness of northwestern Mexico, the Onza was first recorded by the Aztecs as being golden like a cougar, but far more aggressive. When the Spaniards arrived, they recorded similar details, adding that it resembled a wolf and it attacked humans in broad daylight. But it wasn't until hunters Dale and Clell Lee shot a mystery cat in 1938 that we had possible proof of these elusive hunters. Their cat was golden like a cougar, but had longer legs, ears, and tail. Other specimens were killed in the 1970s and '80s, but no sightings have been reported since 1986.

Orang-pendek ••••

"Orang-pendek" means "little man" in Sumatran. The Orang-pendek is generally considered to be one of the cryptids most likely to exist because of the number of sightings and footprints found over the years, particularly by some very reputable people, including villagers, journalists, and conservationists. Sightings go all the way back to the time of Dutch colonization of Sumatra. Expeditions seeking irrefutable proof are ongoing. Witnesses claim that these creatures are between three and five feet tall and are covered with short, dark hair with a thick, bushy mane. Their faces are said to be brown, hairless, and very human-like. Local Kubu villagers also claim that these creatures enjoy tobacco. Other names include *Gugu*, *Sedapa*, *Sedabo*, and *Atu*.

Owlman •••

Similar to the Mothman, the Owlman of England reportedly has been witnessed by many local residents. Three boys said they were chased from a field to the mouth of a metal grate that was just large enough for them but too small for the monster. They described the blood-chilling screams of the frustrated Owlman as it rattled the grate, trying to get through. It supposedly casts a yellow glow as it flies.

Piasa Bird ••

Tales of this winged, fire-breathing "bird" said it attacked villages along the Mississippi River near present-day Alton, Illinois. Over and over, the creature would come and snatch up members of the tribe living up and down the river. Legend says

Chief Outoga of the Illini tribe learned in a dream that the bird was only vulnerable beneath its wings, where they attached to its body. Using himself as bait, Outoga reportedly drew the beast out so skilled archers could shoot poisoned arrows to kill it.

Piltdown Man •

The Piltdown Man is a known hoax that began in 1912 when a skull and jaw fragments were allegedly found in Piltdown Common, England. Because of its primitive look, the "discovery" was called the "missing link" by some proud Englishmen. But experts were skeptical—and with good reason. A second, more authentic skull was found in 1917. By 1953, more accurate scientific tests proved that the 1912 pieces were from a human or an orangutan. No one ever revealed who put the hoax in motion.

Sasquatch ••••

Washington State's Native Americans told tales of a smelly, hairy, man-like giant. The name "Sasquatch" came from their language. Dr. Grover S. Krantz spent his illustrious career at Washington State University and the last years of his life studying Sasquatch, the mysterious, ape-like biped of the Pacific Northwest, because he believed there was enough evidence to make that study worthwhile. Considering tracks that measured up to eighteen inches in length, Krantz believed Sasquatch was a direct descendant of *Gigantopithecus*, a prehistoric ape identified by fossil fragments in China. Based on the length and depths of the tracks, Krantz also believed this evolution would be eight feet tall and might weigh seven hundred and fifty pounds. He once said that if it ever wanted shoes, they would have to be size 28-wide.

Shunka Warak'in ••••

Idaho's Ioway tribe tells of a large, black, dog-like creature that eats small livestock and other dogs. It reportedly has high shoulders and snarling fangs and resembles a hyena crossed with a wolf. Witnesses describe its cry as sounding like a wounded human. Some experts believe it could be the prehistoric canid, *Borophagus*, which is thought to be extinct. One specimen was killed and mounted by a taxidermist in the mid 1900s and was, for a time, on display at a museum in Henry Lake, Idaho.

Skunk Ape or Swamp Ape ••••

A creature found in the marshy, forested areas of Florida, Georgia, and South Carolina, this cousin to Bigfoot has been sighted for decades (if not centuries). It enjoyed a surge in visibility in the 1970s when dozens of reports poured in to local wildlife and law enforcement facilities. Most described a seven- to eight-foot-tall, six-hundred-pound, ape-like biped

(standing on two feet) with light brown hair and a horrific scent—a cross between rotten eggs, manure, and a skunk, inspiring the creature's nickname. In 1997, Ochopee, Florida, fire chief Vince Doerr allegedly spotted the Skunk Ape in a swamp near his home and shot a picture—the first relatively clear image of the elusive animal from the Sunshine State. Campground owner Dave Shealy revealed photos of his own a few years later.

Storsjo, the Lake Storsjon Monster ••••

Although Storsjo was removed from Sweden's endangered species list in November 2005, sightings have been reported since 1635. More recent sightings were taken so seriously that Storsjo—with its snake-like body and dog-like head—was legally protected from hunters for nearly twenty years from 1986 to 2005.

Tasmanian Blob ••••

This mysterious, jellified blob washed up on the shores of Australia's Tasmania in 1960. Originally thought to be the decaying carcass of a sea monster, the blob turned out to be whale blubber, according to the scientific testing that was done in 1962. Other "blobs" have popped up along

beaches around the world, including Chile, Bermuda, Florida, and Massachusetts. Each has proved to be decomposing whale remains.

Thetis Lake Monster •••

If you've seen the classic Hollywood movie *The Creature from the Black Lagoon*, you have a general idea of what this cryptid from British Columbia supposedly looks like. First sighted by two teens in August 1972, it allegedly chased the boys from the shores of Thetis Lake. The Royal Canadian Mounted Police launched an investigation but found little to support the boys' story. Days later, two more people were frightened by a monster similar to the one the boys described—a five-foot-tall, 120-pound bipedal creature with silver scales.

Thunderbird • • •

The Quillayute people of the Pacific Northwest speak of a great bird with a wingspan longer than two war canoes that rescued them from starvation. According to legend, it appeared in the west, carrying a whale. It lowered the whale to the jubilant villagers, and then took to the sky, returning to its cave in the mountains. Other, less kindly thunderbirds have been reported from around the world, including reports from Pennsylvania, Norway, and the Swiss Alps that claimed the thunderbird carried away children and small pets.

Thylacine, Tasmanian Tiger, or Tasmanian Wolf • • • •

Driven to extinction by packs of imported wild dingoes and fearful ranchers, the thylacine is neither a wolf nor a tiger, but rather a marsupial, like a kangaroo or opossum. The females had a small pouch that held their young until they were fully developed. The thylacine had a lean body with stripes on its back and a long tail and could grow to be five feet long. The last verified sighting of a thylacine in the wild was in 1930, but it has been a protected species in Tasmania since 1936 when the last known specimen, Benjamin, died in captivity at the Hobart Zoo in Tasmania. A recent reported sighting makes its extinction questionable.

Tsuchinoko • • • •

This chubby Japanese snake supposedly lives in tall grassy areas and forests. It reportedly chirps, spews venom like a viper, and can jump several feet. It is called "bachi-hebi" in Northern Japan and is referenced in the "Kojiki," the oldest known book about the ancient history of Japan.

U-28 Sea Monster • • • •

When the German U-boat known as U-28 torpedoed the World War I British steamer *Iberian*, it sank more than its human enemies. As survivors floated, awaiting rescue, they saw a sixty-foot-long creature "writhing and struggling wildly" as it took to the air more than one hundred feet up—the result of the Germans' explosion. Within seconds, the creature was gone, but experts speculate that it may have been a prehistoric mosasaur or a crocodilian thought to be extinct for more than 110 million years.

Winged Dragon • • • •

In 1974, police officer Arturo Padilla of San Benito, Texas, saw something strange fly through the beams of his headlights. It looked like a large bird—a really, really large bird. Minutes later, a second officer called in a similar report. A man in Brownsville reported hearing a loud thump, then seeing a bizarre winged creature unlike anything he'd ever seen before. Fossil remains of the great pterosaur, *Quetzalcoatlus*—with a wingspan fifty feet wide—were found in 1970 in Texas's Big Bend National Park, leading to speculation that this mystery animal could be an unexpected prehistoric survivor.

Yeren • • • •

"Mountain ogres" were on poet Qu Yuan's mind more than two thousand years ago when he wrote from his home in Hubei province of China. Hundreds of years later, historian Li Yanshou described a band of "hairy men." Similar stories of tall, upright, man-like creatures covered with reddish-brown hair have emerged across the mountainous region. Some say they retain the powers of speech. Others say they communicate as apes and monkeys do. Speculation that they might be the prehistoric ape, *Gigantopithecus*, or Peking Man, has not been confirmed.

Yeti • • • •

Also known as the Abominable Snowman, this tall, man-like creature resembles Bigfoot but is known to inhabit only the tallest mountain ranges, such as the Himalayas, between India, Nepal, and Tibet. Many sightings by local villagers have been reported through the years but without documented proof. Some reports say the Yeti is gentle, even helpful. Others paint a more dangerous picture.

Yowie • • • •

One of the first documented reports of Australia's Bigfoot was logged during the 1870s. But sightings of have come in from every state Down Under. Australia's indigenous people, the Aborigines, know the Yowie by other names—Doolagahl, Tjangara, Jinka, and Pankalanka—and consider the creature sacred. One report in 1795 described a Yowie running from European settlers as they came in from the bay. Speculation that Yowie still roams the countryside is popular, due to the wide expanses of unexplored, unpopulated Australian territories.

Zuiyo-Maru Monster • • • •

In 1977 a Japanese fishing trawler off the coast of New Zealand allegedly pulled a four-thousand-pound "sea monster" carcass out of the ocean. The decaying body looked like nothing they'd ever seen before. A young sailor who had graduated from an oceanographic high school took five photos, some measurements, and some tissue samples before the crew dumped it back into the sea. Later testing of the evidence suggests the creature was a decaying basking shark. Around the world, decomposing bodies of basking sharks have often been mistaken for plesiosaurs from the past.

Bibliography

Books

Arment, Chad. *Cryptozoology: Science & Speculation.* Landisville, PA: Coachwhip Publications, 2004.

Carmony, Neil B. *Onza! The Hunt for a Legendary Cat.* Silver City, NM: High Lonesome Books, 1995.

Coleman, Loren. *Cryptozoology A to Z: The Encyclopedia of Loch Monsters, Sasquatch, Chupacabras, and Other Authentic Mysteries of Nature.* New York: Simon & Schuster, 1999.

Everhart, Michael J. *Oceans of Kansas: A Natural History of the Western Interior Sea.* Bloomington: Indiana University Press, 2005.

Hall, Dennis Jay. *Champ Quest 2000: The Ultimate Search Field Guide & Almanac for Lake Champlain.* Vermont: Essence of Vermont, 2000.

Krantz, Grover S., Ph.D. *Bigfoot Sasquatch Evidence.* Second edition, revised and appended. Surrey, BC; Blaine, WA: Hancock House Publishing, 1999.

LeBlond, Paul H. and Edward L. Bousfield. *Cadborosaurus: Survivor from the Deep.* Reprint. Victoria, BC, Canada: Heritage House Publishing Company Ltd., 2000.

Newton, Michael. *Encyclopedia of Cryptozoology: A Global Guide to Hidden Animals and Their Pursuers.* Jefferson, NC: McFarland and Company, 2005.

Nugent, Rory. *Drums along the Congo: On the Trail of Mokele-Mbembe, the Last Living Dinosaur.* Boston: Houghton Mifflin, 1993.

Pyle, Robert Michael, Ph.D. *Where Bigfoot Walks: Crossing the Dark Divide.* Boston: Houghton Mifflin, 1995.

Sutherland, Elizabeth. *The Pictish Guide.* Edinburgh, Scotland: Birlinn Ltd., 1997.

Articles

Applebaum, Peter. "A Serpent, or at Least Its Tale, Resurfaces." *New York Times*, October 12, 2005.

Chase, Stacy. "On Bigfoot's Trail: Loren Coleman." *Boston Globe*, February 26, 2006. http://www.boston.com/news/globe/magazine/articles/2006/02/26/on_bigfoots_trail/

Chamberlain, Ted. "Loch Ness Monster Was an Elephant?" *National Geographic News*, March 9, 2006. http://news.nationalgeographic.com/news/2006/03/0309_0603009_loch_ness.html

Ciochon, Russell L., Ph.D. "How Gigantopithecus Was Discovered." University of Iowa Natural History Museum. http://www.uiowa.edu/~nathist/Site/giganto.html

Crawford, Matt. "Fishermen's Observation Re-Stirs Champ Debate." *Burlington Free Press*, August 18, 2005. http://www.burlingtonfreepress.com/apps/pbcs.dll/article?AID=/20050818/NEWS01/508180312/1009

Davies, Adam. "I Thought I Saw a Sauropod." *Fortean Times* 145 (April 2001). http://www.forteantimes.com/articles/145_mokelem.html

"Excitement over Tasmanian Tiger Sighting." *Sydney Morning Herald*, February 28, 2005. http://www.abc.net.au/worldtoday/content/2005/s1312642.htm

Green, David. "Evidence of Jungle Yeti Found." *BBC News*, October 12, 2004. http://news.bbc.co.uk/1/hi/england/manchester/3734946.stm

Holloway, Marguerite. "Beasts in the Mist: David Oren Searches for Giant Sloth in Brazilian Rain Forest." *Discover* 20, no. 9 (September 1999). http://www.findarticles.com/p/articles/mi_m1511/is_9_20/ai_55553382

"Is There a Monster in Lake Champlain?" *ABC News*, February 22, 2006. http://www.abcnews.go.com/GMA/story?id=1648547

Knippenberg, Jim. "Tristater Searches for Giant Sloth." *Cincinnati Enquirer*, May 31, 2001. http://www.enquirer.com/editions/2001/05/31/tem_tristater_searches.html

"Loch Ness Monster May Have Been an Elephant." *Independent Online* (South Africa), March 7, 2006. http://www.int.iol.co.za/index.php?set_id=1&click_id=588&art_id=qw1141678442858B216

Lovgren, Stephen. "Forensic Expert Says Bigfoot Is Real." *National Geographic News*, October 23, 2003. http://news.nationalgeographic.com/news/2003/10/1023_031023_bigfoot.html

Lyons, Stephen. "The Beast of Loch Ness: Birth of a Legend." *Nova Online.* PBS. November 2000. http://www.pbs.org/wgbh/nova/lochness/legend.html

Macy, Richard. "Tiger or Not, They're Photos to Thrill." *Sydney Morning Herald*, March 2, 2005. http://www.smh.com.au/news/National/Tiger-or-not-they're-photos-to thrill/2005/03/01/1109546871418.html

McLeod, James R. "Pend Oreille Paddler: Myth or Mystery." *Sandpoint Magazine* 15, No. 2. Summer 2005. http://www.sandpointonline.com/sandpoint-mag/sms05/feature1b.html

Meldrum, D. Jeffrey, Ph.D. "Evaluation of Alleged Sasquatch Footprints and Their Inferred Functional Morphology." Department of Biological Sciences, Idaho State University.http://www.isu.edu/~meldd/fxnlmorph.html

"More Cressie Sightings in Newfoundland." *CBC News* (Canada), August 14, 2003. http://www.cbc.ca/stories/ 2003/08/01/cressie_nfld030801

Moriarty, Leslie. "Hot on the Tail of Bigfoot: Imprint Thought to Be Beast's Buttocks."*The Herald*, January 13, 2001. http://www.heraldnet.com/bigfoot/story13353257.cfm

Na, He. "'Monster' of Tianchi Lake Sighted." *China Daily*, November 7, 2005. http://www2.chinadaily.com.cn/english/doc/200507/11/content_458959.htm

Naylor, Julie. "Looks More like Big Hoof than Big Foot." *Express News*, University of Alberta, July 28, 2005. http://www.expressnews.ualberta.ca/article.cfm?id=6830

Owen, James. "Holy Squid! Photos Offer First Glimpse of Live Deep-Sea Giant." *National Geographic News*, September 27, 2005. http://news.nationalgeographic.com/news/2005/09/0927_050927_giant_squid.html

"Quebecer Claims to Have Photos of Lake Monster." *CTV News* (Canada), August 20, 2005. http://www.ctv.ca/servlet/ArticleNews/story/CTVNews/1124491024189_22/?hub=Canada

Reuters. "China's 'Loch Ness Monster' Resurfaces." *Sydney Morning Herald*, July 16, 2003. http://www.smh.com.au/articles/2003/07/15/1058035005776.html? oneclick=true

Reuters. "Expedition Sets Out to Trap Norwegian 'Sea Monster.'" *CNN*, August 7, 2000. http://archives.cnn.com/2000/NATURE/08/07/norway.monster/

Richardson-Moore, Deb. "Seeking the Undiscovered." *Greenville News,* August 31, 2003. http://greenvilleonline.com/news/2003/08/31/2003083113295.htm

Schaffer, Ron. "Creature Chronicles: Big Test for Bigfoot Going on at OSU." *Dayton Daily News*, November 6, 1995. http://www.forbes.com/lists/2006/10/1217.html

"Sea Monster or Monster Hoax? Amateur Captures Video of Alleged Lake Beast." *CNN*, June 12, 1997. http://paranormal.about.com/gi/dynamic/offsite.htm?site=http://cnn.com/WORLD/9706/12/fringe/turkey.monster/

"Speculation Mounts over Tassie Tiger Photos." *ABC Northern Tasmani*, March 1, 2005. http://www.abc.net.au/northtas/news/200503/s1312984.htm

"Tourist Claims to Have Snapped Tasmanian Tiger." *Sydney Morning Herald*, March 1, 2005. http://www.smh.com.au/news/National/Tourist-claims-to-have-snapped-Tasmanian-tiger/2005/03/01/ 1109546854027.html?oneclick=true

Wilkerson, James. "Extinct Fish Found in Second Home." *BBC News*, October 2, 1998. http://news.bbc.co.uk/1/hi/sci/tech/185239.stm

Interviews by Kelly Milner Halls

Brewer, Sarina. Owner, Custom Creature Taxidermy Arts. Interviewed February 13, 2006.

Ciochon, Russell L., Ph.D. Professor of Anthropology, University of Iowa Natural History Museum. Interviewed January 27, 2006.

Coleman, Loren. Author and Cryptozoology Expert. Director, International Cryptozoology Museum. Interviewed December 10, 2005.

Everhart, Mike. Author, *Oceans of Kansas: A Natural History Of The Western Interior Sea*. Bloomington: Indiana University Press, 2005. Interviewed November 14, 2005.

Hall, Siobhan. Creative Director, Nimba Creations. Interviewed January 18, 2006.

Kirk, John. President and Editor-in-Chief, British Columbia Scientific Cryptozoology Club. Interviewed January 19, 2006.

Norman, Scott T. President, CryptoSafari. Interviewed December 4, 2005.

Shuker, Dr. Karl P. N. Author and zoologist. Interviewed December 7, 2005.

Simpson, Dr. Yvonne, Ph.D. Geneticist, Edinburgh University. Interviewed November 21, 2005.

Tanner, D. L. Author of cryptozoology fiction. Interviewed January 15, 2006.

Van Otteren, Ed. Wildlife Technician, Georgia Department of Natural Resources. Interviewed March 10, 2006.

Voorhies, Dr. Michael. Paleontologist, University of Nebraska at Lincoln. Interviewed November 15, 2005.

Web sites

American Monsters
http://www.americanmonsters.com

Australian Yowie Hunters
http://www.yowiehunters.com/

Bigfoot Field Researchers Organization
http://www.bfro.net/

Bigfoot: Fact or Fantasy
http://www.rfthomas.clara.net/bigfoot.html

Bigfoot Museum Online
http://www.bigfootmuseum.com

British Columbia Scientific Cryptozoology Club
http://www.bcscc.ca/

Cadbury Australia: Yowie Candy
http://www.cadbury.com.au/sites/cadbury/
    index.php?pageId=84

Famous Canadians: Ogopogo
http://www.canadians.ca/more/profiles/o/o_ogopogo.htm

Champ Monster
http://champmonster.com

Champ Quest
http://www.champquest.com

CryptoMundo: CryptoZoo News
http://www.cryptomundo.com/cryptozoo-news

Cryptozoology.com
http://www.cryptozoology.com

FarShores.com: Altie
http://farshores.org/caltie.htm

Fish Out of Time: Coelacanth Information
http://www.dinofish.com

GA Books: Sightings of the Altamaha-ha
http://www.gabooks.com/sighting.htm

Genesis Park: The Kongamato of Africa
http://www.genesispark.org/genpark/konga/
    konga.htm

Great American Bigfoot Research Organization
http://www.greatamericanbigfoot.com

International Bigfoot Society
http://www.internationalbigfootsociety.com

Lake Hodges Monster
http://www.hodgee.com

LakeNormanMonster.com
http://www.lakenormanmonster.com/home.shtml

Legend of Nessie
http://www.nessie.co.uk

Mokele-Mbembe
http://www.mokelembembe.com

Monster Watch Project
http://www.monsterwatch.itgo.com

Morden Museum, Manitoba, Canada:
    Ancient Sea of Manitoba
http://collections.ic.gc.ca/ancientseas/plesiosaurs.htm

Mysterious World
http://www.mysteriousworld.com

National Library of Australia: Bunyips
http://www.nla.gov.au/exhibitions/bunyips

New Advent Catholic Encyclopedia: Saint Columba
http://www.newadvent.org/cathen/04136a.htm

Nimba Creations Special Effects
http://www.nimbacreations.com

Oregon Bigfoot
http://www.oregonbigfoot.com/patterson.php

Orkneyjar: The Stronsay Beast
http://www.orkneyjar.com/folklore/seabeasts.htm

Orkneyjar: Monsters of the Deep
http://www.orkneyjar.com/folklore/seabeasts.htm

Pyle, Dr. Robert Michael: Biography
http://www.cwu.edu/~geograph/pyle.html

Purvis Lab Orang-pendek Watch,
    Department of Biology, Imperial College, London
http://www.bio.ic.ac.uk/evolve/people/rich/
    pendek.html

Eternal Word Television Network: Saint Columba
http://www.ewtn.com/library/MARY/COLUMBA.htm

San Francisco State University: Brown Throated Sloth
http://bss.sfsu.edu/geog/bholzman/courses/
    fall99projects/sloth.htm

Shuker, Dr. Karl P. N.: Biography
http://members.aol.com/karlshuker

Fortune City: The Strange Case of the Stronsay Beast
http://members.fortunecity.com/yvonneoforkney/beast/
    index.html

Strange Magazine
http://strangemag.com

Texas Bigfoot Research Center
http://www.texasbigfoot.com

TrueAuthority.com: Cryptozoology
http://www.trueauthority.com/cryptozoology/main.htm

Vermont Secretary of State Web site
    Kids' Page: Sea Monsters in Vermont
http://www.sec.state.vt.us/Kids/seamonsters.html

Visit Nepal: Nepal's Bigfoot—The Yeti
    The Mystery of the Abominable Snowman
http://www.visitnepal.com/nepal_information/yeti.php

White Bigfoot Web site and Video
http://www.angelfire.com/oh/ohiosasquatch

The W-Files: An Archive of Wisconsin Paranormal
    Activity
http://www.w-files.com

Index

Abominable Snowman 15, 54, 55
aborigines 14, 18
Affolter, Dick 30
albinism 13
Altamaha-ha 31, 57
American Museum of Natural History 16
Aztecs 46
Bacon, Bennett 31
Barclay, Dr. 23
Barnum, P. T. 50
basking shark 24, 25
Beast of Bodmin Moor 57
Bertin, Jacqueline 31
Bigfoot 5, 6, 8, 10, 11, 12, 15, 16, 17, 18, 19, 20, 21, 37, 55, 57
Bigfoot Field Research Organization 11, 13
Bili (or Bondo) ape 55
Bleathman, Bill 52
Bluff Creek 6, 19
Bodette, Pete 30
Borophagus 47
Brachiosaurus 39
Brewer, Sarina 50, 51
British Columbia Scientific Cryptozoology Club 20
Bunyip 48, 58
Cadbury Yowie 14
Caddy 35, 58
Cardiff Giant 58
Chacoan peccary 49, 58
Champ 28, 29, 30, 59
Chupacabras 49, 59
Ciochon, Dr. Russell L. 16, 17, 21
Clark, Dr. Neil 32
coelacanth 4, 33, 59
Coleman, Loren 4, 19, 21, 54, 55
collared peccary 49
Coltman, Dr. David 12
cougar 46
Davis, Rusty 31
de Champlain, Samuel 28, 29
Devil Dog 47
DNA 12, 21, 38, 52, 55
Dobhar-chú 59
Dover Demon 59
dwarf panda 16

Eastern Ohio Bigfoot Investigation Center 13
elephants 32, 40
Emela-Ntouka 34, 40, 60
Erdman, Mark 33
Everhart, Mike 27
Feejee (Fiji) Mermaid 50, 60
footprints (tracks), 10, 14, 37, 38
Frieden, B. Roy 29
giant ground sloth (Mapinguari) 44, 45, 62
giant octopus 60
giant squid 4, 33, 60
Gibbons, Bill 38
Gigantopithecus 16, 17, 19, 21
Gimlin, Bob 6
Goodall, Jane 20
Grant, Arthur 27
Green, John 11
Hall, Siobhan 18, 19
Halls, Kelly Milner 5
Hartwig, Walter 10
Hellhound 60
Heuvelmans, Dr. Bernard 4
hoax 6, 28, 50, 51, 52
Hutchins, Ross 47
Jenny Haniver 61
Jersey Devil 61
Keating, Don 13
Kirk, John 29
Kongamato 43, 61
Kons, Steve 52
Kraken 61
Krantz, Dr. Grover 11
Kubodera, Tsunemi 33
Lake Champlain 23, 28, 29, 30
Lake Van Monster 61
Lanpo, Jia 16
Lauten, Tom 18
LeBlond, Paul H. 29
Loch Ness Monster 18, 24, 26, 27, 30, 32, 56, 61
Loveland Frog 62
Lynch, Owen 31
Mackal, Dr. Roy P. 41
Mansi, Sandra 28, 29, 30
Mapinguari (giant ground sloth) 44, 45, 62
Marlowe, Dr. Scott 15

Marzoi 62
Mbielu-Mbielu-Mbielu 42, 62
Megalania 62
Megalodon 63
Megalosaurus 23
Meldrum, Dr. Jeffrey 10, 11
Memphré 35, 63
mermaids 51, 63
Mills, Bertram 32
Moa 56, 63
Mokele-mbembe 34, 37, 38, 39, 63
Mongolian Death Worm 63
monitor lizard 41
Mooney, Nick 52
Morden Museum 30
Mori, Kyoichi 33
Mothman 56, 64
Munns, Bill 16, 17
Nandi bear 64
National Science Museum (Japan) 33
Nguma-Monene 34, 41, 42, 64
Nimba Creations, Ltd. 18, 19
Norman, Scott T. 37, 38, 39, 42
Olitu 43
Onza 46, 64
Operation Deepscan 27
Ogopogo 64
Orang-pendek 4, 7, 55, 65
Oren, David 45
Orkneyjar Island 23, 24
Osagawara Whale Watching Association 33
Owlman 65
Pangea Institute 15
Patterson, Roger 6
Peace, John 23
Piasa Bird 65
Picts 26
Pie, Lloyd 19
Piltdown Man 65
plesiosaurs (*Plesiosaurus*) 23, 24, 27, 29, 30
pterosaurs 43
Pyle, Dr. Robert Michael 6
python 41
Regusters, Herman 38
Ringdocus 47
Rock Eagle Museum of Natural History (GA) 31

Romandi-Menya, Steve 43
Royal Museum of Edinburgh 25
Saint Columba 26
Sasquatch 6, 8, 10, 11, 12, 13, 17, 20, 65
sauropod 37, 38, 39
Sherar, George 23
Shiels, Anthony 26
Shunka Warak'in 47, 66
Simpson, Dr. Yvonne A. 24, 25
Skookum Cast 11, 12
Skunk Ape 8, 15, 66
sloth 45
Spaniards 46
Spears, Rick 31
Spicer, Mr. and Mrs. George 26
Stegosaurus 42
Storsjo 66
Stronsay Beast 23, 24, 25, 30, 34
Stronsay Island 23
Swamp Ape 8
Tanner, D. L. 31
Tasmanian blob 66
Tasmanian tiger or wolf 52, 67
Texas Bigfoot Research Center 13
Thetis Lake Monster 56, 66
Thunderbird 67
thylacine 52, 67
Triceratops 40
Tsuchinoko 67
U-28 Sea Monster 67
Vietnam 17
von Koenigswald, Dr. Ralph 16
Voorhies, Dr. Michael 4
Ward, Jennifer 15
Weidenreich, Franz 16
Wenzhong, Pei 16
Wetzel, Ralph 49
white-lipped peccary 49
Winged Dragon 67
Yeren 6, 7, 68
Yeti 6, 7, 15, 17, 24, 54, 55, 68
Young, Roxanne 5
Yowie 6, 7, 14, 17, 68
Zarzinsky, Joseph 28, 29
Zuiyo-Maru Monster 68